THE WORLD OF SERGE DIAGHILEV

Series originated and edited by
Christine Bernard & Charles Spencer

THE WORLD OF SERGE DIAGHILEV

CHARLES SPENCER

with contributions by Philip Dyer and Martin Battersby

Paul Elek LONDON

ISBN 0 236 31054 2

Designed by Pat Ariss
and produced by Paul Elek Ltd.

© 1974 Christine Bernard and Charles Spencer
Published by Paul Elek Ltd.
54-58 Caledonian Road, London, N.1

Filmset by Keyspools Ltd., Golborne
Printed by The Garden City Press Ltd.,
Letchworth, Herts SG6 1JS

Publisher's Note

Philip Dyer, who wrote the first three chapters of this book, played no part in the preparation of the remaining portions, which were written by Charles Spencer apart from the chapter contributed by Martin Battersby.

Acknowledgments

I should like to thank Martin Battersby, who with expert knowledge of the subject has enhanced this book with his contribution on the influence of the Ballets Russes on fashion and Decoration – a subject long neglected. I also thank Miss Joan Lawson for her help in lending material to Philip Dyer. For help with illustrations I am indebted to Messrs. Sotheby's, S.P.A.D.E.M., A.D.A.G.P. The Royal Ballet Covent Garden, the London Festival Ballet, and John Carr Doughty; as well as to the photographers J. S. Lewinski and John Barrow. I deeply appreciate the editorial guidance of Christine Bernard and the devoted secretarial work of Hilda Meyer.

CS

CONTENTS

COVER
Alexandre Benois' setting for Act III of
the ballet *Petrushka*, 1911

LEFT
Diaghilev and his old nurse *c.* 1905,
painted by Léon Bakst in St Petersburg.
Collection Russian Museum, Leningrad

Diaghilev was the creator of an exceptional period of European art. Not only did he introduce Russian painting, music and dance to Western Europe early in the twentieth century, he continued, through the turbulent years of World War I, the Russian Revolution and the hectic twenties, to provide scintillating displays of the highest artistic talent in the West.

Many books on the life of this extraordinary man have been written, ranging from serious biography to scandal-mongering. The man and his career are legendary, yet he remains elusive. 'I, personally, can be of no interest to anyone; it is not my life that is interesting, but my work.' His words supply no clue to the creative method by which his miracles evolved. In charge of an organization which had no consistent financial backing, we have a man seized by the demon of creation, who united prodigious talent in his quest for new artistic horizons – Stravinsky, Bakst, Debussy, Fokine, Picasso, Cocteau, Ravel, Massine, Braque, Satie, Benois, Strauss, Balanchine and Matisse – the list is by no means complete. The responsibility for the way in which these often disparate elements were made to cohere remained his.

Serge Pavlovitch Diaghilev was born on 19 March 1872 in an army barracks in Novgorod, where his father had been posted for a year. The birth was difficult, and his mother survived only a few days. His father was then gazetted Squadron Commander in the *Chevaliers Gardes*, who were stationed in St Petersburg. Like many minor aristocratic families of that period, there were numerous close relatives as well as the additional family created by second marriages, making altogether a complex group. To the general approval of this close-knit family, Diaghilev's father married again after two years.

To this lady, Helene Valerianova Panieva, can be ascribed the cultural foundation as well as the will-power and tenacity of Diaghilev, particularly as his father was frequently away with the army in the provinces. From the beginning she fitted perfectly into the Diaghilev family, generating an atmosphere of ease and comfort. She had a warm capacity for accepting everyone, and whoever came to her home was made an intimate; no distinctions of social prestige or advancement were made between her visitors. Family and friends would participate in operas and song recitals every Thursday evening; their musical knowledge was extensive, the enthusiasm of the adults filtering down to the children so that, quite naturally, it became a necessary part of life. Tchaikovsky was a favourite at a time when his music was relatively little known. The boy Serge was, from his earliest times, greedily absorbing every experience these evenings opened up for him. His lifelong addiction to Tchaikovsky stems from these early days.

Madame Panieve-Diaghilev possessed the highest integrity. At no point was there any discrimination between her own children and her stepson, and to the end of his life Diaghilev always talked of her with the utmost love and admiration. From the earliest times he invariably referred to her as his mother; in this fortunate relationship there was never a hint of the evil stepmother of fiction. She was the first to recognize the inborn abilities of the boy, a sensitivity endowing her with the tact to harness his childish exuberance, tamed only by the most reasoned discipline. It is clear from the history of Serge Diaghilev's career that his stepmother taught him one thing fundamental to his whole life. When, in boyhood frustration, he would cry 'I cannot!' she would answer: 'It is a phrase which you must forget; when one wants to, one always can.'

The Diaghilevs were not exceptional to the concept of upper-class family life at that time. Many minor aristocratic and professional people had similarly enthusiastic cultural patterns. Here it was that the word 'intelligentzia' was created to signify the devotion of a diverse company, ranging from the most privileged to successful businessmen, who gave their leisure and often their fortunes to the pursuit of artistic ideals. Colleagues did not find it peculiar that a merchant would build up a great picture collection or sponsor a music festival. Far removed from the present day use of the word, often distorted now to describe highbrow preciousness, it was originally a term of great respect for amateurs of the arts with high aspirations. Thus it was from the 'intelligentzia' that Serge Diaghilev came. It is impossible to say that at a particular moment he moved from the dilettante to the professional. This was his inheritance, and his entire life became devoted to the discovery of talent and the creation of art.

The young Serge, with his stepmother and the rest of the family, remained in St Petersburg until the boy was ten. His father had improved his position in his regiment, but was seriously in debt to money-lenders. Young Serge's grandfather, Pavel Dimitrievitch Diaghilev, was living with only one unmarried son in a great country house in Perm, offered to pay the debt, provided that his son and the family came to live with him. There it would be comfortable and economical, but it entailed resignation from the *Chevaliers Gardes*. Luckily, although it was an inferior rank, Pavel Pavlovitch was able to secure the post of Commanding Officer of the Reserve Infantry in Perm, thereby saving himself from complete inactivity, as he had no knowledge of agriculture. This turn of events brought an upsurge of life to the property and a new joy to the grandfather. Rapidly the house became the centre of culture for the town. A new music group was formed and a teacher in the Classical High School who was also a proficient pianist played at the concerts that were soon being given by the group. He became music teacher to Serge, continuing his lessons until the boy left school.

The basis for an artistic education was helped as well by grandfather Pavel's collection of illustrated books of the great museums of the world. The atmosphere of the great house and the careful guidance of the family

Serge Diaghilev in his school uniform, aged 18

created an ideal environment for the boy.

He was enrolled in the Gymnasium for his schooling, and from the beginning was given an elevated position by the other students. They were aware that he came from the 'big house' and already possessed a knowledge of music, literature and language. Thus he assumed authority from the beginning. The dreary progress of school days had little to enliven them.. He would come unprepared, yet always managed to get any help he wanted from the more adept pupils. The amazing faculty he displayed in his career for using people when he required them, is visible for the first time in this resourceful behaviour. The teachers themselves gave every possible assistance, for some of them frequented the Diaghilev home. He evidently managed to acquit himself favourably, but the more important part of his life at this period took place at home.

From Perm the family occasionally went to Bikbards to stay with other relatives, and here, apart from the enlivening influence of an even greater number of Diaghilevs, Serge was exposed to the countryside. In later years, when there was the continual pressure of work in cities and the theatre, there was little opportunity to enjoy the pleasures of nature. The mature Diaghilev never forgot the profound effect of those earlier days spent in contemplation of the Russian landscape. They coloured his outlook and determined his fundamental love of all things Russian.

Diaghilev's schooling at the Gymnasium finished when he was eighteen, and he left Perm to continue his education in St Petersburg, where he studied law. There he joined his young cousin Dima Filosofov, already installed, and it was through Dima that he met the group of young men who were to become central to his first creative efforts. The leader of the group was Alexandre Benois, the newest member of a long established Russo-French family of artists and architects, a young man already besotted with the theatre and interested in everything artistic. He was two years senior to Serge Pavlovitch, and at first, with his well-formed cultural background and superior knowledge, was guide and mentor. Walter Nouvel, one year older than Serge, was the gentlest of this initial set of friends; his interests lay in music, history and *belles-lettres*. Although always having a point of view in any discussion, he was not a dominating person, but, like nearly everyone else, he had many quarrels with Diaghilev. Nevertheless, he remained a firm friend until Serge's death.

In his book, *Diaghileff*, Arnold Haskell asked Nouvel for his first impression of Serge Diaghilev upon his arrival in St Petersburg; he was, he said,

. . . a strong, handsome boy, young and in flourishing health, a trifle inclined to fatness. He had wide shoulders, upon which was planted an enormous head out of all proportion to the rest of the body. His hair was thick, and stuck up in bristles like a brush. He had very beautiful large dark brown eyes, that were extraordinarily animated, and a small snub nose very ordinary in shape. His mouth was large, and it became cavernous when he laughed, showing a row of fine teeth. He had fleshy lips, a

Walter Nouvel, Diaghilev's fellow student and life-long friend

low forehead, a prognathous jaw, and a wide chin, that revealed a stubborn will. His complexion was magnificent. His constant animation, his volubility, and the facility with which he expressed himself, his deep booming voice – all denoted a vitality that was infectious. At the same time there was about him something definitely provincial. He lacked that ease and aplomb that distinguished the young man from town.

In *Reminiscences of the Russian Ballet*, Alexandre Benois wrote of his early acquaintance with Diaghilev:

Seriozha remained a newcomer with us for quite a long time. . . . At first we found his presence only just tolerable and nobody took any notice of his opinions. Moreover, he did not frequent our group meetings regularly. He showed himself incapable of following our lectures closely or taking part in any . . . discussions, and showed it so obviously, yawning unrestrainedly to make clear how remote and boring it all was, that at times we became very angry. I used to shout and stamp at him, accusing him of being a thick-skinned Philistine and God knows what else. Seriozha took all this abuse very meekly, without any protest, and would even try to reform himself, being influenced by heart-to-heart talks with his cousin at home. But it was all useless, for the very next time we had our meeting Seriozha would again go to sleep, overcome by irresistible boredom. Diaghilev used further to annoy us by his 'society manners' . . . he made innumerable social calls, leaving cards and putting down his name wherever he could. He was infinitely more refined and careful in his way of dressing than were any of his comrades and even managed to look elegant in our clumsy student's uniform. In short, he tried to represent a real man about town and member of high society. None of us were in the least democratic. We all felt, quite consciously, an absolute indifference to politics . . . and we did not therefore try to penetrate into high society or to 'bow' before anybody. It was loathsome to see Seriozha's ingratiating manner when he approached personalities of high standing in the first rows of the stalls, or when he went his rounds through the boxes in the first tiers. He seemed to assume a special insolence when performing these social 'functions' and this manner of his was attacked and criticized by us so mercilessly that it was surprising how he tolerated it. His behaviour angered and annoyed not only his own friends, but our whole circle of acquaintances. . . . As a student, Diaghilev was never alluded to otherwise than as a 'terrible fop', and this reputation continued to stick to him even in later years, after his merits had become obvious to all. It prevented Seriozha Diaghilev from being taken seriously for a considerable time.

Serge's cousin Dima also joined the group. He was a stylish aristocrat whose mother was a lady of very liberal persuasion, exiled for a period for her political activities. Although reserved, he possessed a caustic wit which masked an inner sentimentality which made him an easy person to dominate. His chief interests were political and social science, philosophy and

Alexandre Benois in Paris *c.* 1895, portrait
sketch by Léon Bakst. Probably in Russia

OPPOSITE

Bakst's design for the letter-heading of
World of Art

literature. At this stage however, the new group were not to be together
for long as Dima and Serge, soon after their arrival in St Petersburg, set out
on their first foreign tour. Although they had to be back in the city for the
autumn scholastic term, they managed to visit Berlin, Paris, Rome, Venice,
Florence and Vienna, the last three cities being for Serge the most important. Dima was the guide and instructor throughout this first excursion. The
rapidity with which Serge assimilated knowledge and refined his taste was
remarkable. From this brief journey he grasped a basic understanding of the
culture of Western Europe far beyond the comprehension of most Russians
of his age. He was to bring this knowledge of foreign ideas and art-forms to
Russia through his periodical *Mir Isstkustva* (World of Art).

Ilya Repin: *The Religious Procession* 1880–
1883. *Collection Tretiakov Gallery, Moscow.*
Repin was the foremost nationalist painter
and an opponent of the foreign influences
introduced by Diaghilev

2 WORLD OF ART

The seeds of cultural revolution were sown in Russia with the publication in 1855 of Tchernichevsky's *The Relationship Between Art and Reality*. To place this event in its historical context, a brief resumé of the artistic heritage of Russia is necessary. The isolation of Russia from Western Europe until the time of Peter the Great gave licence only to the Church to ordain the form of art. The ikon, a formal religious device, had for centuries been a means for both primitive and sophisticated painters to create works of outstanding quality. In time, the Church formulated rules and restrictions on painting, and the ikon degenerated.

After Peter the Great's travels to the West, and his recognition of the gaps in the structure of Russian life, the decision was made to bring the best available talent from Europe to train his people. Soon recognizing this extravagance, he reversed the plan and sent his native talent out to learn techniques new to the rapidly developing homeland. The Tzar's foresight came to fruition during the reign of his daughter, the Empress Elizabeth, when, following the royal example, courtiers built palaces which further embellished Peter's great city. These buildings needed the furnishings of the Western models they emulated, and artists grasped this new opportunity. The first requirement for the decoration of great houses, and a status symbol also, is the family portrait. The artists of St Petersburg fulfilled innumerable commissions, and it was in the form of portrait-painting that Russian art was first successful. Many of the eighteenth-century artists, whose works were scattered throughout the aristocrats' country estates, created great paintings. But it was not until 1905, after incredible research and energy spent travelling over the vast country, that Diaghilev assembled, for the first and last time, more than a thousand of these portraits, many later to be destroyed in the Revolution.

At the end of the eighteenth century aristocratic patronage diminished, allowing an academic formalism to suppress individual talent. The restraint imposed by the Academy during the first fifty years of the nineteenth century became as rigid as the Church's had been towards ikon painting before Peter's reforms; inevitably a lowering of standards resulted.

The message of Tchernichevsky's book was that the artist must fashion his talent to the service of the struggling masses – a theme which has become much more familiar in the twentieth century. There must be a pictorial social alphabet for the millions of illiterates in Russia; this was not the time for Art for Art's Sake, there must be instruction too. This treatise was to lead, a decade later, to the rebellion of the 'Ambulants', a group headed by the artist Kramskoi. Although not himself a great painter, he was a strong

commander of the cause. His edict was: 'It is time that the Russian artist stood solidly on his own feet and rejected foreign influence. Why do we always walk holding the skirts of our Italian nursemaids? It is time to think of creating a Russian school.'

Among this famous group the most notable were: Ilya Repin, who had visited Paris but was antagonistic to the artistic influences there; Vasnetsov, who painted in the heroic style, and is notable for his work on the decoration of the Cathedral of St Vladimir in Kiev, and which he executed in collaboration with two more members of the Ambulants, Nesterov and Vrubel; Benois admired Sourinov while Bakst extolled the virtues of Makovski.

The wealthy mentor of the Ambulants was the Moscow merchant Tretiakov, who assembled their work in exhibitions which visited many provincial towns. The ethos linking their efforts was that Russian art (and subject matter) was for the Russian people the antithesis of the programme inaugurated by Peter the Great. They were representatives of the class struggle, being themselves recently liberated serfs or their descendants. An early communistic group, their survival as a work force would have been unlikely – had Tretiakov not backed their enterprise. As it was, for a further twenty years, until Diaghilev and his friends superseded the group, they completely dominated Russian art.

Outside influences had always entered Russia via Germany, and even up to the time when Diaghilev's friends, led by Benois, became the avant-garde, German art took precedence. Only with the Franco-Russian alliance of 1872 and after the Diaghilev circle started to travel, did Paris begin to supplant Munich. How much greater then becomes the final conquest when, so shortly afterwards, Diaghilev made his triumphant entry into Paris.

This, however, is anticipating later events. When the Diaghilev circle began their crusade with the magazine *Mir Isstkustva* incurring the antagonism of both the academics and the nationalists, their ideals were closer to those of the Academy; without the Ambulants there could have been no possibility of success for the *World of Art*. With the magazine's arrival, and the Nietzschean ethos of the band of friends who made up its editorial board, the important fact to emerge was the absence of any chauvinistic approach. Embodying the widest range of views, these were expressed without class-conscious attitudes. Throughout its existence, *Mir Isstkustva* never contained any political bias, remaining an art periodical devoted solely to art.

Alexandre Benois, writing of the group formed in 1890, the year of Serge Diaghilev's arrival in St Petersburg, claimed:

The real cradle of the *World of Art*, were myself, its elected President, V. F. Nouvel, D. Filosofov, L. S. Rosenberg, who in the following year adopted the name of his grandfather, Bakst, G. F. Kalin and N. V. Skalon. All these were foundation members, and as such enjoyed certain honorary

Mikhail Vrubel: Portrait of Valery Briussov 1905. *Collection Tretiakov Gallery Moscow*. The most gifted Russian painter of his period and a vital influence on the designers for the Russian Ballet

OPPOSITE

Costume design by Vrubel, *c.* 1890, probably for one of Mamontov's productions. *Collection Tretiakov Gallery, Moscow*

16

privileges. Bakst held the office of speaker (and maintained order by means of a brass bell only too frequently employed), and Grisha Kalin was the secretary. As associate members, though not very regular in their attendances, we had C. A. Somov, my childhood friend, V. A. Brun de St Hippolyte, who later vanished completely from our world, J. N. Fenoult, J. A. Mamontov, N. P. Cheremisinov, D. H. Pypin and S. P. Diaghilev . . . Diaghilev himself never lectured, and disliked attending our 'real' lectures, but on less formal evenings he, together with Nouvel, would treat us to pieces for four hands, or would sing in his fine powerful baritone. . . .

Lectures on art, literary talks and musical events were organized, but in spite of high ideals youthful ebullience frequently resulted in erratic attendances, and within eighteen months or so, the Nevsky Pickwickian Society had changed. Benois, Nouvel, Bakst and Filosofov remained; other members disappeared, their places to be taken by Diaghilev, Somov and Benois' nephew, Eugene Lanceray. With them appeared Charles Birlé and A. P. Nourok. Birlé brought a special gift which was to have a far-reaching effect upon the group. This was his tremendous enthusiasm for the 'great' in French contemporary art. He worshipped Gauguin, Seurat and Van Gogh; in literature, Mallarmé, Verlaine and Baudelaire. Nourok, too, contributed his special passion, a keen interest in the work of Aubrey Beardsley.

With these changes in membership, the only 'real' Russians in the group were Somov and Diaghilev; and it was because of the Western attitude to their joint activities that Diaghilev's 'Russianness' frequently caused offence. The others were well aware that, to date, they were far better educated than he. Benois had already noted the somewhat obnoxious social fraternizing which took up much of Diaghilev's time; and although Serge was interested in all their activities, he was not prepared to join in their philosophizing on artistic theory.

Music took priority, in study and in performance with Nouvel, who, with his growing independence, became even more important to Serge. Their friendship grew, and although Diaghilev was very close to his cousin Dima, it was Nouvel who became his *confident*. Together they mourned the death of their hero Tchaikovsky in 1893. Absorption in music seemed complete until, to mark his admiration for Mussorgsky, Diaghilev composed an operatic scene for *Boris Godunov*, for an audience made up of his friends. It was a disaster, after which Diaghilev renounced a musical career forever; with Alexandre Benois as his tutor he then began to take a serious interest in painting.

During the summer of 1893, before the disastrous musical event, Diaghilev and Filosofov paid their second visit to Western Europe, this time paying more attention to Germany. Benois provided introductions to artists of the Munich group, but before they went southwards they spent some time in Berlin where Diaghilev, who greatly admired the work of

Lenbach, bought one of his paintings. In Munich he bought another by Max Liebermann and visited numerous artists with whom he had intense studio discourses. Dima became ill at this time and was sent to the South of France; Serge travelled on alone to Italy, returning to his beloved Venice and Florence, where he purchased a number of antiques, soon to have pride of place in his new St Petersburg apartment. His growing confidence and fierce enthusiasm were matched only by his energetic drive, and in 1895 he again undertook a European tour, this time alone. He bought pictures by Liebermann, Menzel, Bartels and the artist who became one of his ideals – Puvis de Chavannes.

Around this time he visited Jacques-Emile Blanche at Dieppe during the period when a number of English artists frequented the town. 'The first

Léon Bakst in St Petersburg *c.* 1890

time he came' wrote Blanche, 'was in connection with certain portraits he wanted me to paint, of his two cousins, the daughters of the Mayor of St Petersburg. Serge was then a brilliant youth who bought his ties from Charvet, the smartest hosiers in Paris. He was spending his money lavishly, as he always did, and giving wonderful dinners in the restaurants. He created a considerable sensation in Dieppe. Fritz Thaulow, the Norwegian landscape painter, had a villa on the cliff, where he entertained Coquelin, Sarah Bernhardt, Rodin, and all the German and American notabilities who were wandering about France; he asked the young Maecenas from St Petersburg to meet me as well as Beardsley and Conder.'

The St Petersburg group now recognized Diaghilev's educational and intellectual equality, though their numbers were depleted as several of the most informed members and closest friends, including Benois, had gone to live and work in Paris. Diaghilev wrote two articles for the press 'to open the eyes of the public . . . and of our painters', and in 1897, with great success, organized his first exhibition, *English and German Water-Colourists* – a small shaft from the West penetrating the monolith of Russian provincialism. It gave Diaghilev an academic footing so that it became easier, with greater schemes ahead, to improve vital social and financial connections. He paid great attention to his friendship with Princess Tenisheva, and to Sava Mamontov, the Moscow businessman and patron of the theatre.

At the beginning of the following year came a second exhibition, *Finnish and Russian Painters*, at the Stieglitz Museum in St Petersburg. Included were some of the best names Diaghilev could gather; from Moscow, Levitan, Serov, Korovine and Vasnetzov, and members of the Diaghilev group, Benois, Bakst and Somov. The exhibition was a brilliant success for two reasons; the work was of great quality and it was also controversial. Its detractors used the term 'decadent' to totally damn the show. Repin, condemning the Diaghilev circle, said 'It's stupid, it's done for effect'. Igor Graber, in his book about the *World of Art* and the circle of friends, wrote:

In the exhibitions organized by Diaghilev, even before the appearance of the magazine, there could not be found a single picture unintelligible for subject, that might give the public and critics the right to speak of actual 'decadence', or even of 'Symbolism'. All Diaghilev's exhibitions were staged in various ways and the pictures were on the whole much better painted than have been described as the 'miserable productions of "Mussard's Mondays"', 'The Society of St Petersburg Painters', 'The Aquarellists' etc . . . There were no artist-symbolists amongst the Russian participants in the exhibitions of the *World of Art*, nor were there any, at the commencement, amongst the literary contributors to the magazine.

These exhibitions were the prelude to Diaghilev's plans for an art review. The controversy caused by the second exhibition, which aligned artists into different camps and informed members of the public into factions for and against, cast the mould for a magazine different from its original mild conception. Diaghilev immediately realized that it would have to be dynamic, a weapon for attacking the reactionaries and for defending the experimental. A fever of enthusiasm and hard work ensued. The friends were all delighted, and on 18 March 1898, a contract was signed. Princess Tenisheva was the publisher, Mamontov provided the financial backing.

Perhaps the ardour was too great; or was this the first of many occasions when Diaghilev demanded too much of the team? Reaction set in at the moment when everyone was most needed, and the friends drifted away. So Diaghilev and Filosofov alone produced the first issue of *Mir Isstkustva* on 10 November 1898.

The circle of friends had now been together for eight years; from the exuberant and slightly comic over-seriousness of the young, there had grown a body of discerning talent and knowledge of the widest range of interlinking art forms. Growing up together as a group of diverse charac-ters, nurturing an enlightened attitude towards human relationships, the friends had matured into a powerful group, of which the dynamism and authority of Diaghilev now, without doubt, made him the central figure. From this time on it is he who takes precedence. The numerous detractors of these exhibitions were not slow to recognize this growing pre-eminence, reflected in the vehement criticism directed towards him. In the first issue of the magazine, Diaghilev felt bound in his editorial to postulate a creed that was to be maintained:

> Those who accuse us of blindly loving whatever is modern, and of despising the past, have not the slightest conception of our real point of view. I say and repeat, that our first masters and our Olympian gods were Giotto, Shakespeare and Bach, yet true it is that we have dared place Puvis de Chavannes, Dostoievsky and Wagner at their sides. Neverthe-less, this is a perfectly logical development of our fundamental position. Having rejected every accepted standard, each and every one of these artists has been weighed up strictly in accordance with what we, person-ally, demand. We have gazed at the past through a modern prism, and have worshipped only what we, personally, found worthy of adoration.

МІРЪ ИСКУССТВА

V ГОДЪ ИЗДАНІЯ.

САНКТПЕТЕРБУРГЪ
1903.

Cover of one of the issues of *World of Art*,
1903

It was the cult of the individual, vigorously ordered by an informed judgment of art.

The aims of *Mir Isstkustva* were laid down in a brochure accompanying the subscription form:

The review will comprise three sections: The Arts, Applied Arts and Art Chronicle.

Part I will be devoted to Russian and foreign artists of all periods, insofar as their work relates to, and throws light on the contemporary spirit in art.

Part II will particularly devote itself to individual craftsmen, with special reference to outstanding examples of ancient Russian art. With the object of improving the standard of our native industrial art, all Russian artists will be asked to link themselves in this common task.

The literary contributions to both sections will be mainly of a critical nature, covering every art manifestation of interest whether at home or in the West. Exhibitions will be analysed, music chronicled, the latest art journals reviewed, etc.

The controversy surrounding the exhibitions and the birth of the magazine was soon to be blown up to even greater and more hysterical proportions by Ilya Repin, who had a strong influence on the Academy of Arts. For Diaghilev it was immaterial to what group or society an artist belonged provided he himself perceived a great talent; and he was convinced of the merit of Repin.

At the beginning Repin had warmly defended *World of Art*, possibly out of the fear of being thought reactionary. Then successive issues of the magazine began to lambast the work of colleagues, culminating in a fierce demand that mediocre work devoid of historic importance should forthwith be removed from the National Museum. There followed a long list of proscribed artists. Repin was cornered, feeling that it would be unwise to sacrifice a majority of his friends for the new ones of the Diaghilev entourage. He published a letter in the *Niva (The Field)* attacking *Mir Isstkustva* and its allied exhibitions:

Gallén's is the image of the artist gone wild. It is the delirium of a madman, akin to the scrawlings of a savage. Rodin's sculpture bears a close relationship to the stone women found in Scythian tombs in South Russia, while the young Finns, and our own C. Somov, A. Benois, Maliutin, and other half-educated painters, with pious fervour, imitate the mannerisms of those who seek to make ignorance prevail, such as Monet, Rosier, Ancran, Conder, and other contemporary painters.

The creation of the review and its succeeding numbers were achieved against almost insurmountable odds. There was no acceptable typeface – it had to be found in archives; suitable paper for reproductions did not exist; block-making had to be done abroad. The printers were often ignorant as to the use of the blocks and had to be instructed in how to print from them. Dima Filosofov was the dedicated member of the team who took care of this.

The first conflict concerned Victor Vasnetzov, to whom, along with Levitan, Diaghilev and Filosofov decided to devote an issue. The members on the left admired Levitan as a great Russian master, but disliked Vasnetzov's work intensely. The situation was made more difficult by the fact that he was a favourite painter of Mamontov. Dima and Serge defended Vasnetzov as a leader of new Russian art, by inference accusing the others of being devoted only to 'foreign' art. The farcical outcome was that Diaghilev had temporarily to renounce *his* admiration for the French artists, Forain, Helleu and Steinlen! The outcome of this fracas was that Vasnetzov was included, precipitating the threatened resignation of Benois, which immediately brought into operation a typical Diaghilev appeal to friendship, conscience and 'the cause'. Benois stayed. This relatively minor storm is an early example of the particular quality of the young Diaghilev; it was to set the pattern by which he governed his whole career. He established sentimental affiliations which he would destroy when it suited him. When someone opposed him, to bring them into line he would invoke 'conscience' and 'the cause'; and always there was his magnetic power.

Whilst there was constant strife within the precincts of the editorial

The Maryinsky Theatre, St Petersburg in 1890

Portrait of Prince Serge Wolkonsky, Director of the Imperial Theatres, by Ilya Repin. Probably in Russia

24

board, Diaghilev's flat, where the meetings took place, whilst Serge's old nurse presided over the samovar, the world outside was beginning to take note of their combined efforts in *World of Art*.

In 1899 a friend of Diaghilev was appointed to the post of Director of the Imperial Theatres. This was Prince Serge Wolkonsky, who lost no time in allotting important tasks to members of the circle; Diaghilev was made a junior assistant to the Director, Benois was commissioned to design the opera *Cupid's Revenge* by Taneyev, Bakst a French mime-play *La Cœur de la Marquise*, Somov to design programmes, whilst Dima Filosofov was invited to sit on the Committee of the Alexandrinsky Theatre. The Imperial Theatres issued an annual, usually a dull publication; but for 1900 it was a splendid volume as the result of Diaghilev's editing. Included in the volume was an article on Vsevolojsky, the late Director of the theatre, and others on Gonzaga, the eighteenth-century designer and the architect of the Alexandrinsky Theatre. The yearbook particularly pleased the Tzar.

In its second year, the Russian section of *Mir Isstkustva* featured articles by Benois on one of his favourite subjects, the architecture of the eighteenth century, which helped promote societies for the preservation of old St Petersburg. Diaghilev was busy researching what was to be his one published work, a monograph on the eighteenth-century painter D. G. Levitsky. He did, however, also include in the review some pieces extolling modern architecture, indulging the mischievous side of his character, for he was well aware how much it would irritate Benois. In a similar mood there was an essay praising the new American millionaires for their art collecting. However, these occasional irritants were counter-balanced by, at times, an uncommon generosity. Diaghilev, reviewing Benois' book *History of Russian Painting* at about this time, wrote:

Benois' influence on contemporary Russian art is incomparably greater than appears at first glance. If, prejudice aside, it seems to us that the whole future of Russian art now resides in the exhibitions organised under the aegis of the so-called *World of Art* group . . . then it must be admitted that Benois played an all-important part in inspiring that unity and its steadfast convictions. I must confess candidly that though in fact I was the organiser of these exhibitions, but for Benois' influence, the group . . . could never have been rallied to one purpose, for each would have gone his own way. . . . Even as a young man he was always, automatically as it were, inculcating a real love of art in his friends; a love he has never deserted to this day. We are all eternally in his debt for our knowledge, relative though that may be, and for our absolute faith in our mission.

Although in the original prospectus there was the suggestion that foreign contributions would be evenly balanced with features concerning Russian art, with successive issues of the magazine these diminished and finally almost ceased. In the light of history and present-day interest, some of these contributions are noteworthy. In the musical field Grieg wrote on *Mozart and Ourselves* and Nietzsche on *Wagner in Bayreuth*, while articles on foreign painters included Liebermann on Degas, Huysmans on Whistler, Muther on Gustave Moreau, McColl on Aubrey Beardsley, and Ruskin on Pre-Raphaelitism.

Whilst the magazine continued to improve in quality because of greater experience of printing techniques and the regular collaboration of the friends, all of whom were now back in Russia, Diaghilev was engaged in the preparation of the next exhibition, the most elaborate so far, and for the

first time truly international. Alongside carefully selected contemporary Russian and Finnish painters were the best of the Western Europeans. The collection from France, Germany, England and America was authoritative, composed of works by Degas, Blanche, Besnard, Boldini, Renoir, Lenbach, Liebermann, Conder, Brangwyn, Whistler, Alexander and Tiffany. The Tzar and Tzarina, as well as numerous members of the Imperial Family, visited the exhibition; the Grand Duke Vladimir, President of the Academy of Fine Arts – who subsequently became Diaghilev's patron – was genuinely interested and paid several visits.

The second of these exhibitions, also at the Stieglitz Museum, was composed of a wide range of Russian artists admired by the Diaghilev circle, shown with a selection of carefully chosen works of the eighteenth and nineteenth centuries.

Expenditure on these ventures, in addition to the running costs of the magazine, was, not surprisingly, high, and coincided with Mamontov's financial difficulties, who was forced to withdraw his support. At the same time Princess Tenisheva, who had expected to gain more cultural prestige than she actually did as publisher, also retired out of fear of the enmity generated by *World of Art*. Repeatedly throughout Diaghilev's career such crises will be seen to recur; though not really interested in money, he sooner or later (usually sooner) proved himself able to save such situations. On this occasion he permitted a group of friends to guarantee finance for the next year.

OPPOSITE

Carved wooden sideboard designed by Betekof for Princess Tenisheva's art colony at Talashkino

ABOVE

Bookshelves designed at Talashkino

RIGHT

Embroidered chair covers designed by Maliutin for Talashkino. The revival of folk art in Russia in the 1890s, represented in these illustrations, later influenced the designers of the Ballets Russes

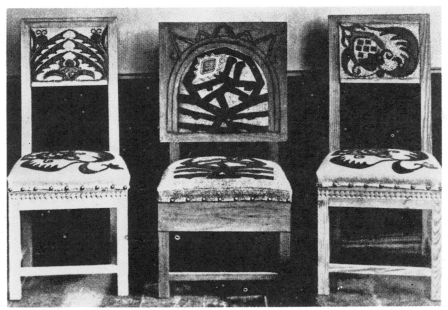

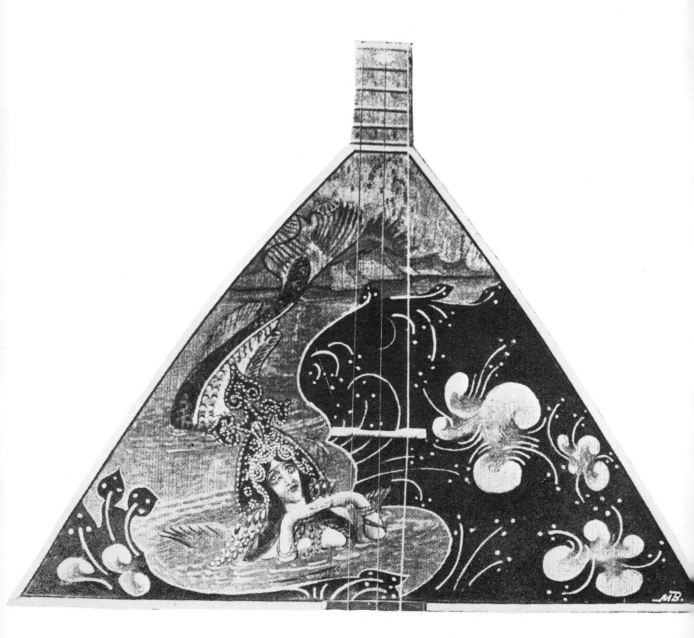

3 WIDENING HORIZONS

In 1901 the third of the exhibitions allied to *Mir Isstkustva* demonstrated Diaghilev's particular authority, whereby, to achieve the finest ambience, no compromise could be permitted (the supreme example of this occurred later when, in almost impossible circumstances, a theatre was completely redecorated in three or four days for the opening of his first season of ballet).

With the help of the Grand Duke Vladimir, and surprisingly Repin, the vast halls of the Academy were secured – to the horror of most of its members. As the walls were covered with bad copies of famous masterworks, Diaghilev organized the erection of small, elegant, well-lit rooms which obscured the offending pictures. Howls of protest arose, the structures were rumoured unsafe – but Diaghilev won.

The Universal Exhibition took place in Paris in the spring of 1900, and Diaghilev was there to see the victory of his East-West endeavours: Serov won the medal of honour, Korovine and Maliutin were awarded gold medals for painting, Golovine and Vrubel for applied art.

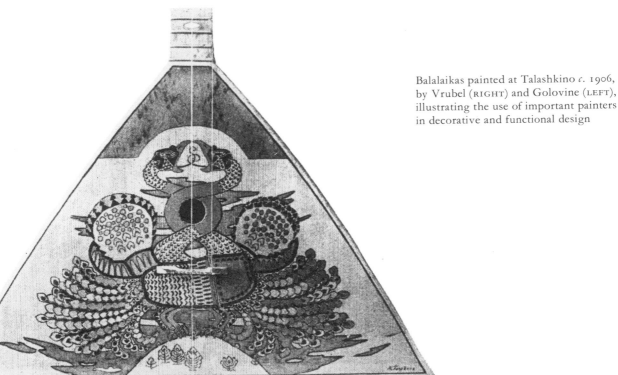

Balalaikas painted at Talashkino *c.* 1906, by Vrubel (RIGHT) and Golovine (LEFT), illustrating the use of important painters in decorative and functional design

Of the artists closely associated with the group Serov, senior in age and
experience, was the most venerated. He was one of the few people for whom
Diaghilev had total respect, deferring to his artistic judgment. He had been
commissioned to paint a portrait of the late Emperor, Alexander III, which
proved eminently successful. There were further requests for royal portraits,
and finally he was asked to paint the Tzar. This portrait, the finest ever
painted of Nicholas II, hung in the Tzarina's apartments in the Winter
Palace, until it was destroyed in the Revolution. The opportunist in
Diaghilev, when funds were again low, took advantage of Serov's close
contact with the Tzar. He suggested that Serov might ask the Tzar to
subsidize the review. This audacious move worked, and the Emperor
guaranteed the magazine for five years.

Although diehards were opposed to everything *World of Art* stood for,
the review was having an powerful effect upon the whole cultural activity
of Russia. The Imperial Society for the Encouragement of Fine Arts
invited Benois to edit a new periodical, *The Treasures of Art in Russia*. It was
arranged that the new magazine would deal only with historical subjects,
thus avoiding any conflict with *Mir Isstkustva*. The musical members of the

circle Nourok and Nouvel, with some friends, founded *Les Soirées de Musique Contemporaine*. Chamber music was all they could afford to perform, but they introduced to St Petersburg remarkable programmes, first performances of Debussy, Franck and Ravel, Schönberg, and Russia's own newcomers, Stravinsky and Prokofiev. Diaghilev was displeased at not being asked to participate, but took it surprisingly well when Nouvel explained that the enterprise had to be modest, and that they were aware that he, Serge, only enjoyed lavish affairs.

The literary set, led by Filosofov and Merejkovsky, founded *Les Assemblées Religieuses et Philosophiques*, and quite soon started their own paper, *The New Path*, exploring religious and mystical trends. Thus, the interest closest to Filosofov at the very start of the Diaghilev enterprise now took over, and his literary editorship of *World of Art* came to an end. Diaghilev asked Benois to be his co-editor, each producing alternate issues.

In the meantime a further exhibition was held at the Arcade Gallery, including a large group of Moscow artists calling themselves 'The Thirty-Six'. The show was highly successful, and a further exhibition was planned for the following year; by then, however, the Moscow artists organized their own. Diaghilev was typically objective, as he always could be about art, praising their exhibition; his own, for the first time, was a comparative failure. For the opening all the *Mir Isstkustva* artists converged on St Petersburg, together with those from Moscow, and an historic meeting resulted, opened by Diaghilev who had been told that some artists had grievances against the selection committee, as well as with the dictatorial powers of Diaghilev. Was it not time then to reorganize and plan future exhibitions on a different basis? Hesitantly opinions were voiced until, gaining confidence, members of *World of Art* joined those opposed to the old regime. The final blow came when Benois too favoured a new society. With the exhibitions brought to an end, it was inevitable that the days of the magazine were numbered, the one being incomplete without the other. The review lasted for one year more, when the Imperial guarantee ran out. Continuation of the Tzar's subsidy was impossible, owing to the enormous expense of the Russo-Japanese War. However, in considering *Mir Isstkustva* as an entity, it must be realized that there were many separate and inter-related events coinciding with those years. Diaghilev was indefatigable, by no means content only to remain at the centre of production of the magazine.

As his stature grew, interest in his activities spread beyond the readership of *World of Art* and the visitors to the exhibitions. His record was sufficiently impressive for him now to be brought into the hierarchy of the Court, as a member of the staff of the Imperial Theatres, though he continued his own art research and work with museums.

The course taken by the Imperial Ballet during the later years of the nineteenth century is important in its effect upon various influential figures

Alexandre Benois: *The Emperor Paul
Reviewing the Troops, St Petersburg,* 1903.
Russian Museum, Leningrad

around Diaghilev. Although the world of the ballet at this time does not yet cross his path, the influences upon some of his friends will have a direct bearing upon his future. One who was thus influenced from an early age was Benois.

Alexandre Benois was interested in everything. His childhood devotion to the magic of theatre had started even earlier than real theatre-going, with the exploration of the annual St Petersburg fairs. Makeshift stages showing harlequinades, puppet shows to be copied at home, strange masked figures of Russian folklore, entranced and sometimes scared the small boy. These experiences, indelibly fixed, were recalled much later when his inspiration set in motion the creation of one of the most famous Russian ballets, *Petrushka*. He was taken first to the Opera Bouffe, where French operettas were performed, to see a children's play. Within a brief period he had seen his first ballet, *La Bayadère*, after which he saw the standard repertoire at the Italian Opera. At that time the ballet was considered by better educated members of the theatre-going public to be superficial, there was nothing to be learnt there, it was merely the indulgence of a limited number of eccentric 'balletomanes'.

Approaching his 'teens, theatre mania increased to the detriment of school, a passion accompanied by parental dismay. For a while he showed little interest in ballet, but at home where the family was large, and where some members were professionally occupied with music, Benois was led more and more to combine his love of the theatre with music. He had temporarily forsaken opera and now ballet caught his attention. At the age of thirteen he recognized that he was a victim of balletomania when he began to idolize the great dancer, Marie Petipa, daughter of the choreographer Marius Petipa. The new addict long afterward considered that her performance in *The Hump-Backed Horse* was the starting point of his lifelong devotion to the ballet. His education in the ballet continued with Delibe's *Coppélia*, from which he made two acquisitions of importance to his future career. Here, as in Tchaikovsky's work, he saw how the easy melodic flow contributed to an inspired full-length work. With this and *Sylvia* Delibes won a special regard from Benois. It will be seen how he tried later to honour this admiration. Then there were the stories by E. T. A. Hoffmann, whose macabre tales were to contribute greatly to his major work for the Russian Ballet.

The dancer who was to have the most profound effect on Benois made her first appearance in St Petersburg very inauspiciously. He knew of her from a magazine, in which she was described as 'the toast of Paris', but he never hoped to see her until he discovered that she was appearing in a suburban amusement park. There he found a pathetically small audience for an elaborately produced operetta, into which, near the end, an inappropriate ballet number had been inserted. Virginia Zucchi danced with such intensity and style that the small audience were enraptured. Word-of-mouth promotion was all there was to recommend her, but soon audiences grew into full houses. Eventually the Tzar expressed a wish to see her, the performance was favourably received, and the outcome was a contract with the Imperial Theatres. There she first appeared in the improbable ballet *La Fille du Pharaon*, but her natural vivacity and spontaneous Italian charm immediately enslaved her audience. Two of the young dancers to be strongly influenced by her qualities and style were the legendary ballerinas to be – Mathilde Kchessinska and Olga Preobrajenska.

When Prince Wolkonsky designated Diaghilev to carry out 'special duties' as one of his assistants at the Imperial Theatres, he had not himself held the Directorship very long. His predecessor was his uncle, Vsevolojsky, who had held the post for seventeen years. The latter, realizing that the Imperial Ballet had been for too long cast in the mould of unchanging traditions had introduced foreign dancers. Vsevolojsky also earned his place in ballet history with his musical reforms. It could be said that most ballet scores at that period were produced by jobbing composers; now he asked a 'real' Russian composer to create works for the repertoire, and Tchaikovsky, the most revered of all at that time, wrote *The Sleeping Princess*, to be followed by *Casse Noisette*. After the composer died in 1893, the previously unsuccessful

Swan Lake was triumphantly revived. A precedent was set, and from that time composers of repute were no longer to disdain the ballet.

Prince Wolkonsky had many of the qualities of his uncle, and his noble background and ardent enthusiasm for the theatre made him eminently suitable to be the new Director. Apart from being acquainted with Diaghilev, and thereby some of the other friends, the Prince's taste and interests paralleled theirs; he was impressed by their work on *Mir Isstkustva*. The wish to appoint members of the group to the service of the Imperial Theatres seemed absolutely right, and the editing of the Year Book by Diaghilev proved his judgment; but in the hierarchy of the Imperial Theatres that was only a beginning.

The permanent staff of the Imperial Theatres were antipathetic to the new Director whom they thought too young. They protested when the 'outsider' Diaghilev was asked to edit the Year Book, and only with some difficulty did Wolkonsky override their disapproval. The fact that the new publication, unprecedented in quality and interest, gained the support of the Tzar, made for jealousy, and Diaghilev himself did not help matters.

Prince Wolkonsky had been impressed by Diaghilev when they first met in relaxed social conditions, but he subsequently had reservations; he learned that Diaghilev could be overbearing, a creator of antagonisms. Whatever he engaged upon, the atmosphere was always stormy. Benois and his friends had found him uncouth when he had first arrived in town, their irritation increasing at his displays of snobbery; but, by now, they had worked together as a team for a long time, at high pressure, devoted to the 'cause' – the magazine and the exhibitions.

Romola Nijinsky's highly coloured best-seller on the life of her husband, published in 1933, paved the way for a more rational account of Diaghilev's life, written by Arnold Haskell with the collaboration of one of the first of the 'friends', Walter Nouvel, published in 1935. To write then of sexual deviation was difficult, particularly when it concerned a celebrated personality, the focal point of a wide group of still-living persons. Times and laws have changed, the realization that sexual behaviour is only one part of the complex of personality and life-style is more accepted than formerly. Moral attitudes no longer create false perspectives as much as they once did.

Prejudice against homosexuality is such, even now, that apologies seem to have to accompany discussion of even the most notable personalities having that inclination. Yet the cultural donation to the western world bequeathed by Diaghilev is so profound that no defensive attitudes are valid. Diaghilev, once his career was established, was to promote, through his love, a few young men whom he believed to have special talent. Those with whom he fell in love were completely possessed, but once the initial sexual curiosity was allayed, the relationship evolved, ardently, into that of teacher and pupil. Each time he wanted his loved one to grow into a supreme artist. He was Pygmalion, lavishing all his knowledge and possessions upon them, eager for every advancement they could make. It could be said that his disappointments in love were only due to human limitations; he wished to create gods, and more than once he nearly succeeded.

Diaghilev's homosexuality was of little importance outside the immediate circle of friends, until this moment of his career when he was given a position of honour in the Imperial Theatre hierarchy. The acclaim given to the Year Book probably added to his arrogance. It did not occur to him that he should be tactful in his dealings with the permanent staff, so easily transformed .into envious bureaucrats. Boorish and autocratic to underlings, he made enemies all the way, especially dangerous in a theatrical organization where unusual behaviour, even eccentricity, is acceptable among those sure of their niche, but where the all-important flaw is rapidly pin-pointed in the misfit. In the way that some homosexuals enrage heterosexuals by their flamboyant disregard of average conventions, he showed no discretion. Gossip mounted (he was presented with a powder puff) to a pitch where, intensely embarrassed, Prince Wolkonsky had to inform Diaghilev that whilst his private life might be his own affair, it must not obtrude to the detriment of the Imperial Theatres.

Diaghilev's group had always had a special place in their affections for the ballet *Sylvia*, and some of them now produced ideas for a new production. The success of the Year Book encouraged Prince Wolkonsky to order Diaghilev to mount this ballet. It was to be a joint effort embracing decorative work by Bakst, Benois, Lanceray, Korovine and Serov. Preliminary sketches and plans were executed. However, the moment the official order was presented a deputation pleaded with the Prince for its cancellation – there would be too much discontent in the 'Establishment' owing to ill-feeling caused by Diaghilev. The order was rescinded, and an outraged Diaghilev threatened his resignation from *World of Art*. This move brought Diaghilev some sympathizers, thereby putting the Prince in a dilemma. At that point, the easier line for him to take was to ask Diaghilev to resign. With ardour Serge refused, and the factions gathered their forces.

Inevitably the affair was brought to the notice of the Emperor who, at first, sided with Diaghilev. His minister, a stickler for protocol, managed, however, to persuade the Tzar to uphold Prince Wolkonsky. The dismissal of Diaghilev was made in a public announcement invoking Article Three, a clause which ordained that a dismissed public servant was unable ever to perform Imperial duties again. The severity of the dismissal aroused the conscience of the Emperor, who, remarking that it was a stupid law, ordered that an alternative post be found for Diaghilev. The post which was found was nominal, in no way tying him down to a set career.

Before the furore of the Diaghilev affair had subsided, Prince Wolkonsky himself had resigned; he had fined his prima ballerina, Mathilde Kchessinska, for a breach of regulations, whereat she brought the power of her privilege with the Court to bear on his departure. The Directorship was given to his Moscow *confrère*, Teliakovsky, a very different personality from the Prince, who looked upon Diaghilev as his most dangerous rival for the Directorship, though he disguised his true feelings by a show of admiration. He feared the critical power of *Mir Isstkustva* and when the magazine showed disapproval of his productions he began to use artists of the St Petersburg group, some being those most admired by Diaghilev's friends. In this way Teliakovsky hoped to create an ambience parallel to Diaghilev's. Thus, while the Director remained secure in his position Diaghilev saw his style purloined and debased in the ensuing productions – though one fortunate result of all this was that Leon Bakst was lured into stage designing, and, to his own astonishment, received great acclaim.

The publication of *Mir Isstkustva* continued in spite of Diaghilev's frequent absence. He travelled a great deal, already concerned with the next projects. He had gained experience in mounting exhibitions in conjunction with the magazine, learning of the gaps and untidiness of the national art collections. A comprehensive plan was forming in his mind for the reform of the entire museum structure and cataloguing, in order to bring the disparate collections to a national unity. This bold scheme had seen the light of day in the form of a report in the pages of the magazine. Grandiose, as so many of Diaghilev's projects were to be in later years, this venture met with no response from the authorities. The research and preparatory work was not wasted however, for out of the disappointment he scored a triumph. He continued his art history research with constant journeys all over the vast country, visiting estates, cajoling the owners of houses everywhere to allow him into attics and cellars. This feverish activity culminated at the time when the magazine expired in 1904. Then preparations began for the historic exhibition of 'Russian Portraits, 1705–1905'.

At the moment when the assembling of the works of art was at the most frantic stage, the first of the terrible warning signals presaging a changing world took place. The abortive revolution of 1905 began with the appalling massacre of 9 January. The seething unrest of the huge majority of the Russian people was already affecting the attitudes of liberals and intellectuals, even those who could not be considered revolutionaries. The gunning down of masses of ordinary people disturbed the consciences of many who had no desire to change the 'Establishment'. A remarkable example of foresight and intuition of what was to come would be seen when the great exhibition opened.

The site chosen for the huge number of works Diaghilev assembled was the Tauride Palace, built by Catherine the Great for Potemkin. Somewhat neglected, away from the main sector of St Petersburg, its history and architecture made an ideal setting for the nostalgic evocation Diaghilev created. He had manoeuvred well. The preliminary announcements showed the Emperor as Exalted Patron, the President of the Organizing Committee H.I.H. the Grand Duke Nikolai Mikheilovitch. Members included Vsevolojsky, the Counts Bobrinsky and Tolstoi, Benois and Diaghilev.

This splendid window-dressing assisted in acquiring the Palace and the loan of exhibits by owners who might have been reluctant to part with their treasures. Benois wrote that 'Seriozha's furious activities were almost frightening at times; one could only marvel at his energy, patience and firmness'.

Benois and Diaghilev were responsible for the hanging, Bakst designed a sculpture court with elaborate *treillage*, in the classic French style, forming a Winter Garden. By the time the huge task was completed, 3,000 paintings and sculptures were in place, given appropriate settings to reflect changing styles and tastes, corresponding to the chronological order of the exhibits. It was the culmination of months of preparation, 200 years of the glory of Russia having been assembled in surroundings as nearly perfect as possible. Any reservations that remained from Diaghilev's career at the Imperial Theatres were brought to an end, for he had created what no other person

The Sculpture Hall in Diaghilev's 1906 Russian Exhibition at the Grand Palais, Paris. Bakst's setting was originally devised for the exhibition of Russian Portraits in St Petersburg the previous year

could have done.

A banquet was given in his honour; he might have expressed his thanks in a conventional way. He did not. His speech was an exposé of his position, past, present and future, in a world which was to change completely, and at the very place from which he spoke:

The honour that you have shown me in today's gathering is as pleasant as it was unexpected. Having heard only yesterday of the projected meeting, I was deeply moved, and I felt that I was not ready to receive such a touching expression of attention for everything that we have done, suffered, and achieved. . . . Don't you feel that this long gallery of portraits of big and small people that I have brought to live in the beautiful halls of the Tauride Palace is only a grandiose summing-up of a brilliant, but almost dead period of our history? Impregnated as I am with the aesthetic point of view, I am as moved by the theatrical brilliance of the eighteenth century as before the legendary brilliance of the sultans of the eighteenth century, but these fairytales I remember only from old wives' tales . . . we cannot any more believe the romantic heroism of terrifying helmets and heroic gestures.

I have earned the right to proclaim this loudly, because with the last breath of the summer breezes I ended my long travels across the immensity of Russia. It was just after those acquisitive expeditions that I became convinced that the time to sum up was before us. I saw that not only in the brilliant portraits of those ancestors, so far removed from us, but more vividly from their descendants, who were ending their lives. The end of a period is revealed here, in those gloomy dark palaces, frightening in their dead splendour, and inhabited today by charming mediocre people who could no longer stand the strain of bygone parades. Here are ending their lives not only people, but pages of history . . . We are witnesses of the greatest moment of summing-up in history, in the name of a new and unknown culture, which will be created by us, and which will also sweep us away. That is why, without fear or misgivings, I raise my glass to the ruined walls of the beautiful palaces, as well as to the new commandments of a new aesthetic. The only wish that I, an incorrigible sensualist, can express, is that the forthcoming struggle should not damage the amenities of life, and that the death should be as beautiful and as illuminating as the resurrection.

But Diaghilev, at this moment of triumph was suddenly faced with a series of blows. His long friendship, now fifteen years old, with his cousin Dima Filosofov came to a bitter end in a homosexual quarrel. In gratitude for his splendid work Diaghilev was offered a court appointment, but felt too proud to accept. His name was submitted for the post of his choice, but it was rejected. Teliakovsky was firmly placed in the Imperial Theatre Directorship, leaving no opportunity for Diaghilev there. He left for Paris with his secretary Mavrine, already aware that Russia was high fashion with the French. He discussed ideas for a new exhibition in Paris with Benois, then living at Versailles with his family, and cemented powerful relationships with influential people, before returning to St Petersburg, confident about his next venture. Space was secured in the Grand Palais for 1906, the Grand Duke Vladimir was made President, and, as before, an imposing array of names formed the committee. The Russian Ambassador to France headed the list, which included the Comtesse de Greffulhe, a lady who was to remain a close friend and faithful ally. Diaghilev's official title was *Commissaire General de l'Exposition*. With Bakst to assist him, he began to select treasures of Russian Art. The exhibition would include works from the earliest ikons to the most recent paintings. Many of the artists commended in *Mir Isstkustva* were represented. Most exhibits belonged either to Imperial collections or to the great private patrons. Only with the grandest of aspirations and so·prestigious an event could the loans have been effected. Diaghilev had become Russia's Cultural Ambassador.

Bakst created the decorative background for the galleries of the Grand Palais, repeating his trellissed sculpture court. Benois produced an illustrated catalogue which included a text on Russian art history. Diaghilev was one of the first to present different art forms together. Quite conventional today when 'mixed media' programmes are a norm, in 1906 it was extraordinary. Diaghilev wished to show all the best that Russia could provide, and so arranged concerts of Russian music at which the great Felia Litvinne sang in the brocade-hung galleries. The impact of the exhibition upon the French was such that he was offered the Legion d'Honneur. It was typical of Diaghilev to suggest that the honours should be presented to Bakst and Benois.

LEFT

Golovine's design for the
Imperial Theatres, St Petersburg —
Gluck's *Orpheus*, Act III, Scene 1, 1900.
Collection Tretiakov Gallery, Moscow

OPPOSITE

Chaliapin as Boito's Mephisto. Artist
unknown. *Collection Philip Dyer, London*

4 THE BALLETS RUSSES—EARLY YEARS

Little was known in Europe of Russian music until the turn of the century, except by composers and performers who had visited St Petersburg or Moscow, though leading French musicians knew of the Russian 'Five' (Balakirev, Ciu, Borodin, Mussorgsky and Rimsky-Korsakov), as well as Glinka.

It is altogether appropriate that in his role as unofficial Russian cultural ambassador Diaghilev should have sought to 'export' music after art. He was by training and inclination himself a musician, and Walter Nouvel supported this interest, in preference to other art forms. As Benois wrote in his *Memoirs*: 'We did not need to worry about Russian literature, for during the last thirty years it had gained universal recognition . . . but there remained music which in our opinion was not yet sufficiently appreciated.' For a concert season of *Russian Music Through the Ages*, with a typically imposing committee including Nikisch, Glazounov, Rachmaninov and Rimsky-Korsakov, five concerts were designed as a resumé of nineteenth-century and contemporary music; they included works by all these composers as well as by Liadov, Tchaikovsky and Scriabin. Compositions now regularly played in concerts throughout the world received their first performances in the West at those evenings at the Paris Opera in 1907. Perhaps the greatest 'sensation' was the singing of Feodor Chaliapin who instantly became the leading basso in the world. Despite this however, according to Benois the concerts 'met with rather indifferent success'.

This factor, plus the success of Chaliapin, decided Diaghilev to bring a complete opera to Paris in 1908 – Mussorgsky's *Boris Godunov*. Thus for the first time the West not only enjoyed Russian music and Russian singing but was given a glimpse of the standards of contemporary Russian production. The decor was by Golovine, Juon and Benois, with magnificent costumes by Stelletsky. The sumptuousness of the ensemble was largely due to the capacity for taking pains and for orchestrating different talents which Diaghilev was to display to such effect in later years. In St Petersburg, whilst the scenery was being painted on the stage of the Hermitage Theatre, Diaghilev himself chose the materials for the costumes, using his rooms as a warehouse. He visited second-hand markets with Benois and haggled with colourful Tartar and Jewish merchants for the eighteenth-century kerchiefs which ended up as brilliantly embroidered collars on the boyars' costumes.

When *Boris Godunov* came to Paris Misia Sert (then Madame Edwards) was immensely curious about Diaghilev, whose exhibition of Russian painting had been so successful and 'whose fame was growing'. The opera made an enormous impression on her. 'I left the theatre stirred to the point

of realising that something had changed in my life.' She even went so far as to buy up all the unsold seats, since, she says, 'Paris was not yet attuned to Russian music'. Once again, however, despite the attendance of leaders of Parisian society and cultural life, and critical acclaim, the eight performances of *Boris* were not a commercial success. Nevertheless, for Diaghilev it was the third successive annual triumph in Paris. He had gained enormously in self confidence and assurance, winning a host of influential and wealthy friends in the French capital. Misia Sert became his closest woman friend throughout his life and the Princesse de Polignac his greatest patron.

These factors must be taken into account in trying to understand why Diaghilev then turned to ballet, in which he had not previously taken much interest. His ambition had been fully aroused – not only to repeat his successes, but to fully extend his genius as an impresario. As early as 1895 he had written to his stepmother a letter containing this now famous assessment:

> I am, firstly a charlatan, though rather a brilliant one; secondly a great charmer; thirdly frightened of nobody; fourthly a man with plenty of logic and very few scruples; fifthly, I seem to have no real talent. Nonetheless, I believe I have found my true vocation – to be a Maecenas. I have everything necessary except the money – but that will come.

It is interesting to note that in the English magazine *The Studio* (October 1906) Gerald Siordet, writing of the Russian exhibition at the Salon d'Automne, refers to Diaghilev as 'a St Petersburg *maecenas*'. Perhaps Diaghilev himself promoted the description he had arrived at eleven years previously.

If Diaghilev wished to prove himself – and he most certainly did – to the Russian establishment which had denied his genius, and if he wished to continue to reap the rich satisfaction of his Parisian successes, he realized that such objectives could not be achieved in mere art exhibitions or further demonstrations of Russian music alone. It soon became clear that the most potent instrument to hand was the superb ballet company at the Maryinsky Theatre, of which the young Pavlova, Fokine and Nijinsky were already shining stars. It was perhaps Benois who brought the greatest pressure to bear, although throughout his career Diaghilev always arrived at decisions for entirely personal reasons. Benois was not only a life-long devotee of ballet, but had in 1907 created with Fokine *Le Pavillon d'Armide* for the Maryinsky. The possibility of its presentation in Paris inspired Benois to influence Diaghilev.

Another close friend and artist, Leon Bakst, who had contributed so much to the success of the *World of Art* magazine and exhibitions, had also by this time revealed his great theatrical talent in the 1903 ballet *La Fée des Poupées* at the Hermitage Theatre, and in a series of classical Greek productions. Added to this Diaghilev could now count on the support of the Grand Duke Vladimir, uncle of the Tsar, who had backed the production of *Boris Godunov* and was willing to obtain further funds for his more ambitious plans. Other factors included the acclaim already achieved outside Russia by Anna Pavlova, Lydia Kyasht, Bolm and other Russian dancers as soloists or as members of troupes in European theatres and music-halls.

According to Gabriel Astruc, who was to become Diaghilev's French impresario, the genesis of the project to bring ballet to Paris lay in his conversation with Diaghilev after one of the performances of *Boris Godunov* in 1908. Astruc admired the dancing in the Polish scene, which promoted Diaghilev to extol the glories of the Imperial Ballet in St Petersburg and especially the virtuosity of Nijinsky, Pavlova and Fokine. When Astruc urged that he should bring them to Paris, Diaghilev questioned whether whole evenings of dance would succeed. There was also the question of cost. The impresario assured him that this was no problem; the next day, according to Astruc, a contract was signed and he obtained financial guarantees from a group of banking friends, including Henri de Rothschild, Basil Zaharoff and Arthur Raffalovitch.

Diaghilev suggested bringing the ballets *Le Pavillon d'Armide* with Pavlova, *Sylvia* and *Giselle*. He also listed possible patrons for the season, including Princesse Murat, Princesse de Polignac, the Comtesses de Chevigné, de Pourtalés, de Hohenfelsen, de Castellaine, and Baroness de Rothschild. Of these ladies it was the Princesse de Polignac who emerged as Diaghilev's principal patroness.

Back in St Petersburg Diaghilev set about making his plans, relying on the collaboration of his old friends of the *World of Art*. By this time he was a great personality in the capital. Even the Tsar was impressed with his success abroad, and rumours that he was to include ballet in future presentations aroused great interest. Serge Grigoriev, then on the staff of the Maryinsky Theatre (as indeed were most of the future members of the Ballets Russes), later recorded in his book, *The Diaghilev Ballet 1909–1929*, that at this stage Diaghilev began to attend performances of ballet. One day, he relates:

> Fokine with whom I was great friends told me that Diaghilev had not only at last decided to give ballets as well as operas during his Paris season, but had invited him, Fokine, to become his Maître de Ballet . . .
> and then a few days later Fokine said that Diaghilev wished to know whether I too would join them as regisseur.

In these capacities Fokine and Grigoriev were invited to join the famous 'Committee'. Meetings took place in the dining room of Diaghilev's apartment in St Petersburg. Round the oval table sat Benois, bearded and wearing pince-nez, the elegant and perfumed Bakst, with his curious guttural accent, General Bezobrazov, Privy Counsellor and balletomane, the famous critic Valerien Svietlov and Walter Nouvel, one of Diaghilev's earliest friends, a great music connoisseur. Diaghilev's secretary, Mavrine, made up the group, and his valet Vassili, successor to the old Nanny of earlier years, served tea from the samovar on a side table.

At successive meetings of the 'Committee' other friends who happened to call were invited to take part in the discussion – the painter Serov, the connoisseur Prince Argutinsky-Dolgorukov, Dr Sergei Botkin, Tcherepnin the composer, and others. The scene takes on the informality and intimacy of a Chekov ensemble, with its mixture of friendly banter and egocentricity.

Diaghilev's original intention was a programme of operas plus the ballet *Le Pavillon d'Armide*. The death of the Grand Duke Vladimir, Diaghilev's principal Russian backer, led to the withdrawal of official support and the Imperial subsidy. This in turn led to the refusal of the famous ballerina Kchessinska, and the dancer Gerdt, both favourites at Court, from offering their services. Diaghilev searched for other financial backing. At one stage

OPPOSITE TOP

Walter Nouvel, 1914, portrait by Constantin Somov. Both Nouvel and Somov were members of the *World of Art* group

OPPOSITE BELOW

Portrait head of Fokine by Emmanuele Ordono de Rosales. *Collection Philip Dyer, London*

LEFT

Pavlova and Nijinsky in *Le Pavillon d'Armide*, probably the original Maryinsky production prior to the 1909 version for Diaghilev. *Photo courtesy John Carr Doughty*

45

he borrowed one thousand pounds from Walter Nouvel for three months –
but took a year to repay it. He also took to 'selling' titles to Russian businessmen – a practice long used in political circles, including the British. Eventually he obtained help from friends in Paris, but it was necessary to reduce
the costly operatic programme. Nouvel, who refused to believe that ballet
would succeed in Paris, urged the total cancellation of the project. The
Paris Opera itself objected to the ballet performances and in the end the
famous 1909 debut took place at the Théâtre du Châtelet.

The final programme was the whole of Rimsky-Korsakov's *Ivan The
Terrible* with Chaliapin, plus single acts from *Russlan and Ludmilla* by
Glinka and Borodin's *Prince Igor* – the latter of course including the famous
Polovtsian Dances.

According to Grigoriev, 'Diaghilev's chief interest was centred on the
opera, the performances of which were to be the main event of the season';
the ballet was no more than an extra, chosen to make up four separate
programmes of music and dance. According to Benois, 'It was the choice of
ballets that presented the biggest problems'. Like the operas, however, this
was largely dictated by the existing repertoire. In addition to *Le Pavillon
d'Armide*, a second successful Fokine ballet, also designed by Benois, was
chosen – *Les Sylphides* (originally *Chopiniana*); and then a third Fokine
work *Egyptian Nights*, re-cast, with Diaghilev's typical disregard for
niceties, as *Cleopatra*. To the original score by Arensky Diaghilev un-
heedingly added bits by Taneyev, Rimsky-Korsakov, Glazunov and
Mussorgsky – ending with what Nouvel described as a 'mediocre Russian
salad'. The fourth ballet, another hotch-potch of music, choreography and
designs from the Maryinsky repertoire, was called *Le Festin*. Referring to

ABOVE

Fokine in the Polovtsian Dances from
Prince Igor, 1909

LEFT

An impression by A. E. Marty of the
Polovtsian camp in *Prince Igor*, 1909, from
the magazine *Comœdia Illustré*

this predilection for revisions or adaptations, Walter Nouvel explains that Diaghilev 'always laid stress on dramatic effect, he was terrified of boring his audiences and on that account never hesitated to make cuts that musicians and critics might consider sheer vandalism'. Apart from Fokine as the principal choreographer and male dancer, the company was headed by Pavlova, Nijinsky, Karsavina, Bulgakov, Baldina, Bolm and Federova. Ida Rubinstein, a beautiful young stage-struck Jewish heiress, who at Bakst's instigation had been taking lessons with Fokine, was engaged for the part of Cleopatra – much to the disgust of the ballet-purists on the 'Committee'. In fact Ida Rubinstein and *Cleopatra* were the greatest hits of that momentous first season at the Châtelet in 1909.

The old building was completely renovated with new carpets and lighting and several rows of the stalls were removed to house the orchestra. At rehearsals in St Petersburg, Diaghilev told the company: 'I am delighted to

ABOVE

The first performance of *Les Sylphides* in Paris, 1909

LEFT

An early photograph of Ida Rubinstein (seated), probably at the Maryinsky Theatre, St Petersburg, with Fokine (?) in striped blazer, next to Bakst and perhaps Bronislava Nijinska. This may have been during rehearsals for *La Nuit d'Egypt*, later adapted as *Cleopatra*

47

A rare photographic record of the Russian
dancers in Paris, 1909, during a break
from rehearsals for the first historic season

be showing Paris the Russian ballet for the first time. Ballet to my mind is one of the most lovely arts and exists nowhere else in Europe . . .' Rehearsals meant the end of 'Committee' meetings. All decisions were taken in the theatre. Diaghilev supervised everything. According to Grigoriev: 'He would frequently argue with the scene painters about a particular tone of colour in the scenery or with the costumiers about some stuff of which a costume was to be made, always obtaining what he wanted.'

The company rehearsed under Fokine in the Catherine Hall, eating their meals together. Benois felt that the happy atmosphere of these preparations for the first Paris season 'had much to do with its subsequent success. It gave the whole company fresh vitality'. The Maryinsky season ended on 1 May; the next day the company were en route to France. In Paris preparations went ahead for the opening night on 19 May 1909. The young Jean Cocteau was commissioned to produce an illustrated brochure and every device was used, as usual with Diaghilev, to excite the press and the public. Serov's poster, showing Pavlova in ballet dress, appeared all over Paris, announcing the *Saison Russe* at the Châtelet in May–June. Diaghilev's friends and backers regularly turned up at rehearsals – often to Fokine's annoyance – and with many personal friends, artists, writers, musicians, crowded into the dress rehearsal on 18 May. In *Le Figaro* the critic, Robert Brussel, who incidentally claimed that as early as 1906 Diaghilev assured him that he would bring the Russian ballet to Paris, described preparations for the opening night:

> The whole company had assembled at the theatre to-day – the ladies from Moscow who work in short tunics of green Liberty silk and those from St Petersburg who are already in tutus. . . . The thin highly strung young man who looks like a fencing master . . . is Michel Fokine . . . Among the men is the extraordinary Nijinsky. . . .

On 19 May both the company and the public were in a state of feverish excitement. Astruc ensured that the house represented *tout Paris*, plus its feminine charms:

> It was my principle to look after the auditorium on my first nights as if it had been part of the scenery. In May 1909 the evening of the revelation of the Russian Ballet, I offered seats in the front row of the First Balcony to the most beautiful actresses in Paris. Out of fifty-two invitations fifty-two answered *Yes*. I took the greatest care to alternate the blondes and brunettes, and as everyone came on time when the Stage Manager gave his three knocks, a smile of satisfaction lit up all those pretty faces and the whole house burst into applause.

The newspaper *Le Temps* noticed this innovation on its front page, referring to the bevy of pulchritude as Astruc's *corbeille* (basket), the name given to French theatre balconies ever since.

Astruc and Diaghilev took as much care in 'dressing' the house as the ballets; the world's leading opera houses were represented, as well as most governments; the *haut monde* dazzled the audience from their boxes, led by

the Comtesse de Greffuhle and Robert de Montesquiou; Paquin and Doeuillet led the world of fashion; Rodin, Blanche and Forain the world of art; Ravel, Fauré, Saint-Saëns music; while the large theatrical contingent was variously queened by Cecile Sorel, Yvette Guilbert and Rachel Boyer. Isadora Duncan was there to witness her influence on Fokine. The young Cocteau confirmed his reputation as an *enfant terrible*. One member of that unique first-night audience, the poetess Anna de Noailles, recorded its effect:

> When I reached my box – and I arrived a little late, for I did not believe in the sensation foretold me by some of the initiated – I realized that a miracle confronted me. I could see things that had not lived before. Everything dazzling, intoxicating, enchanting, seductive, had been assembled and put on that stage. . . .

As Arnold Haskell has written: 'The accounts of those first Paris performances have passed into history'. Diaghilev and his Company became the rage of Paris and the whole season was an indisputable triumph. As Serge Lifar later put it – 'There is no word to express the sacred flame, the frenzy with which the whole audience was seized'. Nijinsky in particular was immediately acclaimed as a genius – a full-page photograph of him in *L'Illustration* bore the caption 'Dancer Nijinsky more talked of than debates in the Chamber'. Of the women, however, it was Ida Rubinstein who emerged unexpectedly as the star. 'Her engagement had been something of a gamble' according to Benois, but she proved to be the 'big trump card in our Paris success'.

That first Paris season set the seal on immediate developments. Diaghilev realized that the public responded enthusiastically to the virtuosity of the

dancers, notably Nijinsky, with whom he was now in love. The beauty, strength and grace of the male dancers acted as an erotic thrill on Parisians of all sexes. This not only excited Diaghilev's personal taste, but, as in the case of Pavlova, aroused some resentment from the ballerinas. The French audiences also responded to the magnificence of the decor and costumes, above all when allied to the exotic rendering of sex and violence in *Prince Igor* and *Cleopatra*. The latter ballet also established Leon Bakst as the company's leading scenic artist.

Bakst, responding to the strange beauty of his *protégé* Ida Rubinstein, devised an extraordinary entrance for the Egyptian Queen, vividly recalled by Jean Cocteau:

There appeared a long ritual procession. First, musicians who drew from

OPPOSITE

Poster for the first Russian Season in Paris 1909, based on Valentin Serov's drawing of Pavlova

LEFT TOP

Bronze figurine by Phillipe, probably based on Ida Rubinstein in *Cleopatra*. *Collection Leslie Esterman, Brighton*

LEFT

Ida Rubinstein in her costume for *Cleopatra*, 1909

their tall oval lutes full mellow chords, like the breathing of reptiles . . .
then followed like figures in terracotta fauns with white manes, and slim
maidens with sharp elbows and eyes without profiles, and all the
equipage of a royal galley. Finally, balanced on the shoulder of six
stalwarts a kind of chest of gold and ebony. . . .

From this chest a swathed mummy was lifted by four slaves who unwound a
series of brilliantly coloured veils to reveal the glorious figure of Cleopatra
' . . . and so she stood, with vacant eyes, pallid cheeks and open mouth,
before the spellbound audience, penetratingly beautiful like a great pungent
perfume of some exotic essence'. The ballet critic and historian Valerien
Svietlov concluded: 'The first season of the Diaghilev Ballet must be com-
memorated in letters of gold . . . to say it was successful is to say nothing. It
was a revelation, a major event in the artistic life of Paris. . . .'

The company were invited to perform at the Quai d'Orsay for the Corps
Diplomatic, at a garden party given by Baron de Rothschild, and even at the
Opera which had originally turned down the season. The French Govern-
ment awarded the *Palmes Académiques* to Pavlova, Fokine, Nijinsky and
Grigoriev. 'Looking back on our weeks in Paris' Grigoriev recalled, 'all of

ABOVE

Benois' setting for *Giselle*, 1910, reproduced from *Comœdia Illustré*

RIGHT

Cover design by Paul Iribe for Jean
Cocteau's magazine *Schéhérazade*, inspired
by Rimsky-Korsakov's music before the
1910 première of the famous ballet.
Collection Charles Spencer

us, Diaghilev included, could scarcely believe that what had happened was true'. But Diaghilev refused to commit himself to another season: '. . . We shall see, we shall see . . .'

Back in St Petersburg his fame and reputation led to new rivalries and jealousies, as well as new offers of support. He warned the 'Committee' that

a second Paris season would require new ballets, not borrowings from the Maryinsky repertoire. Paris had made it clear that what it wanted was excitement – not the re-vamping of classical themes. Diaghilev therefore turned down a suggestion to re-stage *Giselle*. He wanted a ballet to Rimsky-Korsakov's symphonic poem *Schéhérazade* and a version of the Russian fairy tale *The Firebird*. When the composer Liadov was unable to undertake the score, Diaghilev remembered a young composer, Igor Stravinsky, whose composition *Fireworks* he had admired. The story is told of Stravinsky being summoned to Diaghilev's apartment after the concert. The young composer grew impatient after a long delay and was just about to leave when Diaghilev entered the hall and greeted him. In later years Stravinsky pondered – 'How different would my life have been if I had opened that door and disappeared'.

The programme was balanced with a more romantic piece, *Le Carnaval*, which Fokine and Bakst had already staged for a charity performance in St Petersburg; and then Diaghilev created one of his typical divertissements, *Les Orientales*, which had the virtues of being both exotic and using a selection of attractive music, as well as showing off the company's star

A scene from *Schéhérazade*

OPPOSITE TOP LEFT

Nijinsky in his costume for *Les Orientales*, 1910

OPPOSITE BELOW

Kissilev as Shah Zeman in *Schéhérazade*, 1910

OPPOSITE TOP RIGHT

Nijinsky as the Golden Slave in *Schéhérazade*, 1910

performers. In the end, largely under Benois' insistence, *Giselle* was added to the programme. It was the only flop of the season and Diaghilev was justified in his original doubts. However, Benois was not present to witness this failure because of the first of many serious rows with Diaghilev and Bakst. Throughout the history of the Ballets Russes Diaghilev constantly played these two artists, who were among his oldest friends, against each other. They were rivals for his favours and commissions, and were thus the subjects of a sadistic delight.

Benois insisted that the story for the ballet *Schéhérazade* was his idea, although members of the 'Committee' always found it difficult to dis-

57

entangle authorship from their hectic discussions. When the programme for the second Paris season appeared Bakst was listed as both author and designer of *Schéhérazade*. Diaghilev brushed aside Benois' objections with the remark that as he already had one ballet to his name – *Le Pavillon d'Armide* – why shouldn't dear *Levushka*!

What seems like ruthlessness or insensitivity on Diaghilev's part was really only a reflection of communal creativity. The critic Svietlov explained:

Diaghilev's new ballets are quite a different matter. Painters, composers, choreographers, writers and people belonging to the artistic world in general, all meet and discuss their future plans. Somebody makes a suggestion, others back it or reject it, in fact it is hard to say who is the

real author of the libretto, which is thus created by common discussion. The real author is the man who had the original idea; but then everybody helped to develop it. After this the next point for common discussion is the style of the music and the dancing. The painter most inspired by the subject undertakes the decor; he creates the setting, costumes, accessories, down to the smallest detail. That is why the ballet gives such an impression of unity in its idea and its production. The painters, who have devoted their whole lives to studying problems of style, period, modelling, colour and line (all things which the choreographer has never had a chance to study at leisure), ought to be his ceaseless helpers on an equal footing. After learning from the painter what groups are likely to create the most powerful effect on stage and the most attractive design, the ballet master can use this as a background for his choreography.

(It was, in fact, the painters who attracted most attention in Paris, the decors being the true novelty. Whilst the dancers were admired, little notice was taken of the choreography).

The 'Committee' system did not last. Increasingly Diaghilev became dominant; if not exactly dictator, then the only one with the authority, the right to make final decisions, to instruct even the most distinguished composer or artist that some change or other was necessary for the total concept of the work. The basis for this authority, at least over the dancers, has been explained by Tamara Karsavina:

> As a young man he already had that sense of perfection which is an undeniable attribute of genius. He could distinguish temporary truth in art from eternal truth. At the time I knew him he was never wrong in his opinions, and the dancers had implicit faith in his judgment.

The second season in Paris May/June 1910 was an even greater success than the 1909 programme. Whilst *Carnaval* surprised the audience with its romantic simplicity, it was *Schéhérazade* which both astounded and satisfied them. Above all it raised the name of Leon Bakst to star quality. He revolutionized theatrical design, and his daring use of colour launched new fashions and influenced interior decoration for more than a decade. As late as 1925 a ballot held in London listed *Schéhérazade* as the most popular ballet in the repertoire. The same ballet also confirmed Ida Rubinstein as a theatrical personality, inspiring her to launch out on an independent career.

Schéhérazade represents the quintessence of Diaghilev's first period – the Russian oriental phase, with its combination of sumptuous design, sex and violence. The decor itself in Paris provoked prolonged applause at each performance; and the orgy scene, when the ladies of the harem take advantage of their husband's absence to indulge themselves with a band of muscular negroes, aroused cries of uninhibited delight. Similarly, when the culprits were discovered and the Sultan took his bloody revenge, the audience was driven into ecstasies. (Whenever Misia Sert wished to give the painter Renoir a treat, she would take him to the Ballets Russes: 'Schéhérazade aroused wild enthusiasm in him'.)

OPPOSITE

Karsavina in her costume for *Le Carnaval*

ABOVE

Marty's impression of *Le Carnaval*, drawn for *Comœdia Illustré*, 1912

Firebird, also in the 1910 programme, was of greater importance as the first complete Diaghilev ballet – Stravinsky having been commissioned to write the music and to collaborate directly with the choreographer and designer. It launched the composer on his international fame and close friendship with Diaghilev, which over twenty years resulted in a series of masterpieces. Diaghilev's belief in Stravinsky, often against critical and public opposition, is one of his greatest memorials.

As yet Diaghilev's dancers were not a permanent troupe. They were drawn from Russian companies in Moscow and St Petersburg during the vacations. Rehearsals had to be fitted in when dancers were available. Finance, Diaghilev's responsibility; was precariously based on friendships and patronage. It was impossible to recoup costs since the impermanence of

PPOSITE

da Rubinstein in her costume for
chéhérazade, 1910

IGHT

Karsavina and Fokine in *The Firebird*,
910

The underwater sequence in *Sadko*, Paris
1911

OPPOSITE LEFT

Bakst's costume design for Nijinsky as *Le
Spectre de la Rose*. *Private Collection.
Photograph courtesy Sotheby's*

OPPOSITE RIGHT

Jean Cocteau's caricature of Nijinsky
being revived after the final leap in *Le
Spectre de la Rose*. The onlookers include
Bakst, Diaghilev, and Misia and José-
Maria Sert

OVERLEAF

One of Bakst's costume variations for *The
Firebird. Collection Galleria del Levante*,
Milan

the company prevented long foreign tours. However, in 1911 a supposed
accident resulted in the formation of the Ballets Russes. With Diaghilev
accidents were always fortuitous. They invariably resulted in the fulfilment
of his inspirations, or scandals which enhanced his fame. In 1910 he
informed the 'Committee' of his intention to form a permanent company.

> It seems senseless to me to go on assembling a fresh company every year
> only to perform in Paris for a short season. Our very success proves that
> abroad there is a demand for ballet and that we should be all but certain
> to succeed. After taking everything into consideration therefore I
> propose founding for the first time a large private company. . . .

The major difficulty was the dancers. The 1911 scandal with Nijinsky
solved that problem. Nijinsky's resignation from the Imperial Theatres
gave Diaghilev an international favourite around whom a permanent company could be created, ensuring bookings and audiences abroad. The story
goes that at a performance of *Giselle* at the Maryinsky Theatre Nijinsky's
costume shocked a member of the Royal family, which resulted in the
dancer being fined, and then handing in his resignation. There are many
versions of this story, some reporting Nijinsky's omission of his jock strap

others that Diaghilev had Bakst shorten his tunic. Diaghilev, with his usual nose for publicity, immediately cabled Astruc in Paris:

Reason costume Carpaccio designed Bakst. Monstrous intrigue . . . appalling scandal. Use publicity.

As Prince Lieven, one of the most reliable historians of the Russian Ballet, puts it, 'The possibility of the whole scandal being a clever tactical manoeuvre of Diaghilev is not to be ignored'. Indeed this soon became general opinion; even Proust, who had originally sent a telegram of sympathy, later remarked, 'If he (Nijinsky) hasn't been victimized then *merde* to him'.

By this time Diaghilev and Nijinsky had formed their close relationship. Walter Nouvel rather naughtily told Diaghilev, 'How odd it is that Nijinsky should always be the slave in your ballets' (referring to *Pavillon d'Armide*, *Cleopatra* and *Schéhérazade*). Nouvel added the rider that he hoped one day Diaghilev would emancipate the slave.

The tragic story of Nijinsky has been told many times. As a dancer of extraordinary virtuosity he belongs to both history and legend. He was certainly one of the principal factors in the early success of the Ballets Russes, but had Diaghilev not fallen in love with him it is doubtful whether

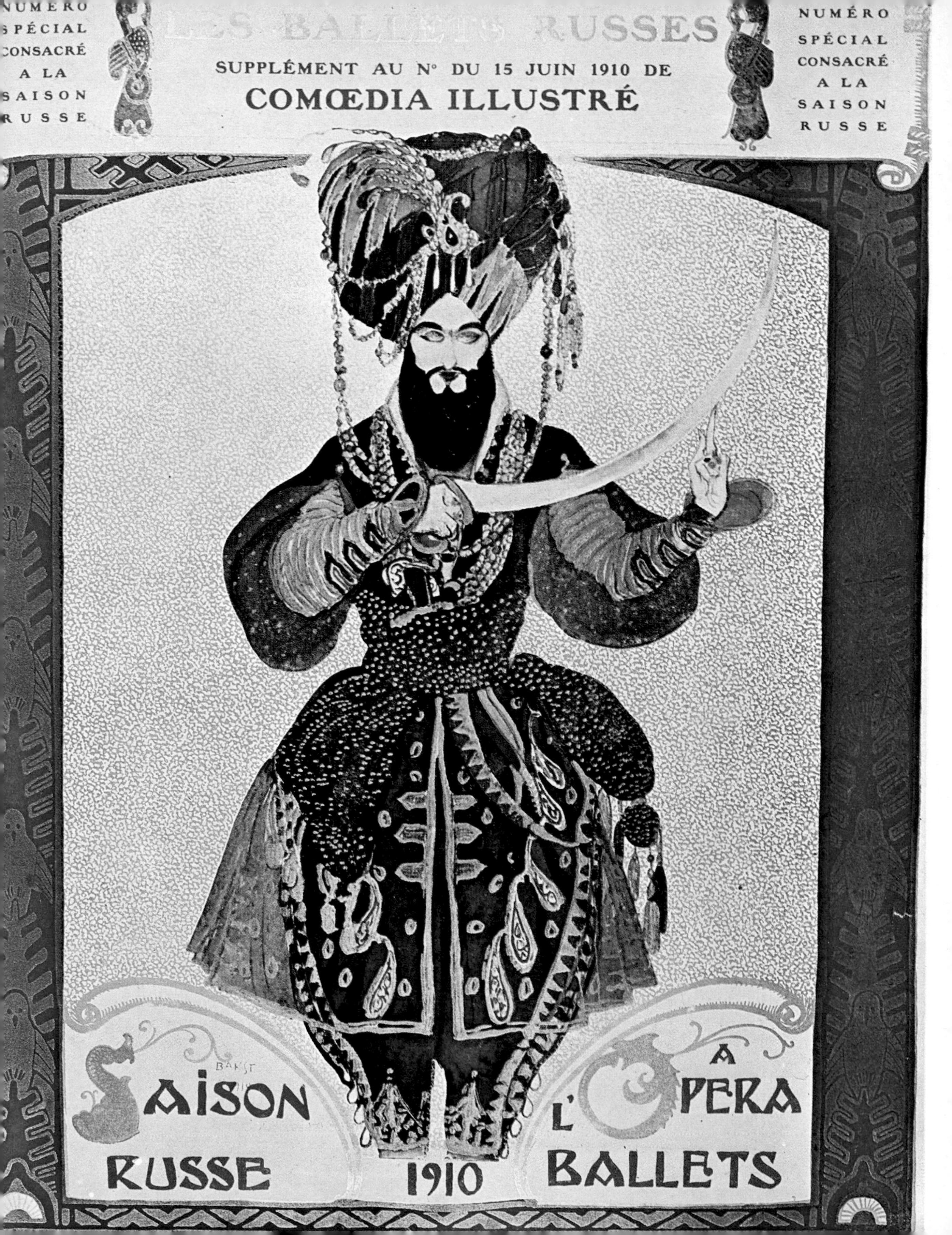
LES BALLETS RUSSES
NUMÉRO SPÉCIAL CONSACRÉ A LA SAISON RUSSE
SUPPLÉMENT AU N° DU 15 JUIN 1910 DE
COMŒDIA ILLUSTRÉ
NUMÉRO SPÉCIAL CONSACRÉ A LA SAISON RUSSE
BAKST
SAISON RUSSE
1910
A L'OPERA
BALLETS

PREVIOUS PAGE

Cover of the Ballets Russes supplement of
Comædia Illustré, 1910, based on one of the
costumes for *Schéhérazade*

this strange youth would ever have been projected onto the international
scene. Certainly no one but Diaghilev would have tried to make him into a
choreographer. One can but surmise whether such over-zealousness did
not unhinge an already disturbed personality.

But to return to the events of 1911. With Nijinsky now under contract
Diaghilev could virtually attract any talent he desired – except, as it happens,
Pavlova, who formed her own company and, in her own way, probably
popularized ballet even more than Diaghilev. Although her standards were
lower she exerted an amazing talent and personal magic in bringing ballet
to modest audiences all over the world.

In the new company Fokine insisted on the title 'Choreographic Director'
in an attempt to stem Diaghilev's boosting of Nijinsky. The season which
opened in Paris on 6 June 1911 included a series of new works – *Le Spectre
de la Rose, Narcisse, Sadko, Petrushka*, plus a new version of the Maryinsky
Swan Lake, in which the famous prima ballerina Kchessinska was
partnered by Nijinsky. Otherwise Karsavina replaced Pavlova as the
company's leading female dancer. Except for *Sadko* Nijinsky appeared in all
the new works, as well as most of the existing repertoire. The abiding
success of the season was *Petrushka*. The idea for a ballet inspired by a
Russian carnival was Stravinsky's. For the decor Diaghilev performed his
usual act of contrition with Benois, who since *Schéhérazade* had refused to
work with him. Perhaps even more successful was *Le Spectre de la Rose*. The
idea came from Jean Vaudoyer in a letter to Bakst. The French critic had
quoted from Theophile Gautier's poem *Le Spectre de la Rose*, in a review of
Carnaval, and now proposed a ballet on the subject. It provided one of
Nijinsky's greatest parts, exploiting his peculiar a-sexual personality and
amazing hovering elevation. According to Jean Cocteau:

> He had noticed that half of the leap which ends *Le Spectre de la Rose* was
> invisible from the house. He invented a double leap by which he curled
> up in the air backstage and fell perpendicularly. They caught him like
> a boxer with warm towels, slaps and water which his servant Dimitri
> threw in his face.

Petrushka exploited the other side of Nijinsky's genius, his pathetic,
despairing nature. *Narcisse* the first of a series of famous Greek ballets,
although in itself of little mark, again depended on Nijinsky's sexual
ambivalence. Cocteau was constantly infatuated with Nijinsky, and altogether found the paederastic milieu round Diaghilev much to his taste.
Unlike Stravinsky, who once declared:

TOP LEFT

Gontcharova's set for *Le Coq d'Or*, Act I,
from the Souvenir Programme 1914

BELOW LEFT

One of Bakst's *Demi-Divinités* for *Narcisse*,
and two of Benois' costumes for
Petrushka, from *Comædia Illustré*, 1911

> It is almost impossible to describe the perversity of Diaghilev's entourage
> – a kind of homosexual Swiss Guard . . . I remember a rehearsal . . . in
> Monaco . . . at which our pianist . . . suddenly began looking very intently
> beyond the music rack. I followed his gaze to a Monagesque soldier in a
> tricorne, and then asked what the matter was. He answered, 'I long to
> surrender myself to him'.

After Monte Carlo the company journeyed to Rome before opening in

Paris. It was in Italy that Stravinsky completed the score for *Petrushka*. Fokine was restive – the enormous task of rehearsing the old ballets, often with new dancers and creating so many new works, was becoming too much. When Grigoriev intervened, Diaghilev retorted:

> That's nothing to do with me. Fokine shouldn't have wasted his time rehearsing the old stuff. He should have worked at Monte Carlo on *Petrushka*; and he must find time now even if he has to keep at it morning, noon and night.

It was typical of Diaghilev to convey complaints and bad news through an intermediary – usually the loyal Grigoriev. It was he in later years who signed the telegram dismissing Nijinsky, and conveyed similar news to Massine.

Diaghilev was anxious over presenting his own company in Paris. The Parisians expected excitement. *Narcisse* they found tame, but *Sadko* was more to their taste, whilst *Le Spectre de la Rose*, with its mixture of acrobatics and sexual symbolism was an immediate hit. The real test of the season was *Petrushka* and Diaghilev invited a young Frenchman, Pierre Monteux, to conduct Stravinsky's music – a wise precaution since at the first rehearsals the music provoked much orchestral mirth. Rehearsals went badly, largely because of friction between Diaghilev and Fokine. Diaghilev was also to prove once again tactless to Benois. The decor had been damaged in transit, especially the portrait of the conjuror. Little did Benois realize that Diaghilev disliked this portrait and was determined to have it changed. Benois was unable to repaint the damaged picture because of illness, and Bakst, under instructions from Diaghilev, offered to do it. Then, writes Benois:

> How great was my surprise at the dress rehearsal two days later when I saw instead of 'my' portrait of the conjuror a totally different one, showing him in profile with his eyes looking sideways . . . I considered the alteration of my portrait an unpardonable outrage against me as an artist, and my whole plan for the ballet. Last year's insult came immediately to my memory. My fury expressed itself in a loud shout across the theatre, filled with a highly select audience.

Benois resigned his post as Artistic Director, refused to attend the first night of his greatest success, and renounced his intention of going to London.

London, in fact, had long been on Diaghilev's itinerary. In 1908 he had turned down an offer from a leading music-hall. He then obtained an option on Drury Lane, but this fell through. In the meantime Sir Oswald Stoll, a

An impression of *Petrushka*, from *Comœdia Illustré*, 1912

fervent balletomane, had attempted to import the Russian Imperial Ballet and in June 1909 Karsavina and Theodore Kosloff led a small company to London. Even before that Lydia Kyasht and Bolm had danced at the Empire, and soon Pavlova was to make her English debut.

The first visit of the Ballets Russes to London was under impressive auspices – sponsored by the Marchioness of Ripon, Diaghilev's most influential English friend, and under contract to Sir Joseph Beecham, whose son Thomas was to conduct. The season at Covent Garden was opened on 21 June 1911 and on 26 June the company contributed *Le Pavillon d'Armide* to the Coronation Gala of George V. The subdued reception on that occasion in no way reflected the success of the Ballets Russes in London. Despite the shocked reaction of some of the public to the physical passion in many of the ballets, *Cleopatra* and *Schéhérazade* became firm favourites. The romantic works were also popular, but Diaghilev waited two years before introducing the more advanced music of Stravinsky to London. The unqualified acclaim of the press and the public – 'Many people are postponing their departure from town in order to see them out', reported the *Sunday Times* – as well as the box-office returns, encouraged Beecham to

Karsavina, Orlov and Nijinsky in the original production of *Petrushka*, 1911

70

LEFT

Stravinsky with Nijinsky in his costume for *Petrushka*

ABOVE

Studio portrait of Tamara Karsavina, from the 1919–1920 Official Programme of the Ballets Russes

book the company for a longer visit in October.

With a permanent company at his disposal and a growing repertoire, the enormous expense of the whole enterprise decided Diaghilev to undertake more tours. After conquering Paris, Monte Carlo, Rome and London he was anxious for Russia to see the ballets of Fokine, the superb decors, and especially Nijinsky. Failing to book any of St Petersburg's theatres, he took Narodny Dom (People's House), which unfortunately burned down before the season took place.

(In his book on *Nijinsky*, Richard Buckle refers to a telegram addressed to Astruc stating that Diaghilev had booked Mata Hari to appear with the company in Russia – a curious home-coming gift! Mata Hari was staying at the Ritz Hotel: 'One day she approached Diaghilev and asked if she could join the company'. After Diaghilev's refusal the lady continued to write renewing her offer. Some time later, at the French border, when asked by the police about his association with the notorious spy, he explained that except for this casual encounter at the Ritz he had had no connection with her.)

Writing of Diaghilev's relationship with the company, Arnold Haskell comments:

> To 'own' a troupe was particularly suited to Diaghilev's aristocratic outlook, and he took an immense pride in that troupe, and a deep active interest in the welfare of its members. He could always be as charming to subordinates as he was sometimes difficult with his equals. However he expected a very high standard of work and this was immediately noticeable by the hush and extra effort when he walked into the rehearsal rooms, and altogether his presence in the theatre meant a far better performance. It was for him they always danced.

Portrait study of Lydia Lopokova, from the 1921 Official Programme

Ninette de Valois talks of him as 'A great man, an autocrat, he could be incredibly kind yet extremely unfair. . . .' Another English dancer in the company, Lydia Sokolova (originally Hilda Munnings) says:

> You did everything you were told. I remember dancing two principal parts and being expected to dance in *Firebird*, in the corps de ballet, as well. I asked if I needn't do that as I needed the rest. With those veiled eyes of his he said, 'You will dance what you are told to dance. It is an honour for you to dance in my corps de ballet'.

This story shows Diaghilev in much the same light as that described by the Russian composer Nabokov. With the exceptions of Stravinsky, and in the early days Benois, Nabokov says, 'Everybody else in his ballet was part subject, part object, used for his aims'.

In his book *The Russian Ballet in Western Europe 1909–1920*, the English writer W. A. Propert defined 'experience and audacity' as essential qualifications for leadership. He continues:

> Government by autocracy is the only conceivable rule under which such a company as Diaghilev's could prosper; and autocratic he certainly is at times. But through all the long stages that precede the birth of a new

ballet he is wise enough to merge the autocrat in the counsellor . . . to see Diaghilev at a rehearsal is to know an altogether different side of him and to realise that behind the easy-going dilettante lies the stern master director.

On one occasion Diaghilev outlined his views on ballet:

> The more I thought of that problem of the composition of ballet, the more plainly I understood that the perfect ballet can only be created by the very closest fusion of the three elements of dancing, painting and music. . . .

When interviewed on the origins of his own company, he added:

> I had already presented Russian painting, Russian music, Russian opera in Paris, and from opera to ballet was but a step. Ballet contained in itself all these other activities.

Typical of Diaghilev's extravagance was the second London season in November 1911, when the great Kchessinska appeared in *Swan Lake* with Nijinsky, accompanied on the solo violin by Mischa Elman – who doubled this performance with a recital at the Albert Hall.

73

RIGHT

RIGHT

Karsavina in *Le Dieu Bleu* 1912

BELOW

Jean Dulac's caricatures of Stravinsky, Bakst, Ravel and Fokine, for the Souvenir Programme, 1912

OPPOSITE

Bakst's decor for *Thamar*, 1912. *Collection Galleria del Levante, Milan*

74

1912 was a momentous year in the annals of the Ballets Russes, the beginning of its cosmopolitan as against Russian character, the break with Fokine, the emergence of Nijinsky as choreographer, leading to the break with Nijinsky himself. In that year four ballets were added to the repertoire – *Le Dieu Bleu*, *Thamar*, *L'Après-midi d'un Faune* and *Daphnis and Chloe* – all designed by Bakst, himself destined shortly to fall into disfavour. The year included performances in Berlin, Dresden and Vienna, and a meeting with Jacques Dalcroze whose theory of eurhythmics was to influence Nijinsky's choreography. After Vienna the company visited Budapest, another fateful halt, since it was there that the young Romola first saw Nijinsky dance, and decided to marry him.

Back in Monte Carlo the company began to prepare its new programme. The public still expected the old flavour of oriental sex and violence. Thus *Le Dieu Bleu* and *Thamar* were chosen, because, says Grigoriev, 'The exotic flavour of such works was precisely what appealed to the public, and . . . "Lyovushka" might be depended on to captivate Paris once again with the wonderful decor'.

The failure of the two ballets resulted in an even greater estrangement

75

with Fokine. By this time it was known that Nijinsky was working on *L'Après-midi d'un Faune*. It will never be established just how much the ballet was his, or Diaghilev's, or Bakst's – or indeed Nijinsky's sister Bronislava's. Preparations were in secret and rehearsals protracted. Diaghilev created an unprecedented stir of expectancy and publicity for the new

Baron de Meyer's famous montage of *L'Après-midi d'un Faune*, 1912

ballet, which had its premiere in Paris on 29 May 1912. Influential friends were welcomed at the rehearsals and expected to spread the news all over Paris. Soon everyone was talking about it. The performance involved another of Diaghilev's scandals. The ballet ends with the Faun finding the nymph's scarf, to which he makes love. Diaghilev was warned there would be a public outcry, but refused to alter a step.

At the premiere there was the usual dazzling audience, including the aged Rodin, for whom Nijinsky had posed, arousing Diaghilev's ever-active suspicions. As predicted, when Nijinsky laid his body on the scarf and enacted a series of erotic jerks, there was an outraged reaction from part of the audience. Characteristically, Diaghilev promptly ordered the whole ballet to be repeated. The next day *Le Figaro* denounced the 'loathsome' performance, and in due course Rodin as well as the painter Odilon Redon and others came to Nijinsky's defence. Of course it all resulted in wonderful business at the box office.

It also provoked Fokine's resignation, infuriated with the publicity given to Nijinsky and upset that his own Greek ballet *Daphnis and Chloe*, long delayed, was only to be given at the end of the season. Diaghilev, writes

George Lepape's sketch of Nijinsky for the special number of *Comœdia Illustré*, 1912

76

Nijinsky as the Faun

ABOVE RIGHT

Jo Davidson's relief of *L'Après-midi d'un Faune*, from the Souvenir Programme 1912

RIGHT

Two bronze studies of Nijinsky by Rodin, *c. 1912. Left, private collection; right, collection Dr and Mrs Henry Roland. Photographs courtesy Arts Council of Great Britain*

77

Grigoriev, received this decision with indifference: 'I had come by now to realise that he valued his collaborators only as long as, in his view, they had something new to contribute. Once they ceased to fulfil this role he felt no regret in parting with them.'

Diaghilev was determined to establish Nijinsky as a great choreographer. His second effort, *Jeux*, was given at the Théâtre des Champs-Elysées on 15 May 1913. It had the distinction of being the first ballet in modern dress, based on a game of lawn tennis and, as *L'Après-midi d'un Faune*, with a score by Debussy. The ballet added nothing to Nijinsky's reputation.

More important was Stravinsky's *The Rite of Spring*. Once again Diaghilev virtually pushed Nijinsky into the role of choreographer. Romola Nijinsky writes: 'This complicated ballet needed infinite time. Nijinsky warned Diaghilev that he would require a great number of rehearsals, as he developed the technique, and that the steps would be extremely difficult to execute.' A young pupil of Dalcroze, Marie Rambert (as she was later named), was engaged to work with Nijinsky. Rehearsals were endless since Nijinsky had the greatest difficulty in instructing the company. The dancers began to hate the ballet, whilst Nijinsky himself became increasingly remote. The first performance produced one of the most riotous premieres in theatrical history. Grigoriev writes:

> Not many minutes passed before a section of the audience began shouting its indignation; on which the rest retaliated with loud appeals for order. The hubbub soon became deafening; the dancers went on, and so did the orchestra, although scarcely a note of the music could be heard. The shouting continued even during the change of scene, for which music was provided; and now actually fighting broke out among some of the spectators . . .

The *Comœdia Illustré* reported:

> Violent interpolations against the young school of modern composers . . .
> against the murmurs and sneers of the sophisticated audience assembled
> at the gala representing a house worth Fr. 35,000, the composer exclaimed
> 'They are ripe for annexation' . . . in a moment of calm a voice from the
> Balcony shouted 'the artists cannot hear the music'. . . . It was Serge
> Diaghilev who with Olympian calm consoled the dancers and insisted
> that they continue. . . .

The effect upon Nijinsky was shattering, the second time one of his ballets
experienced such a reception. However, when presented at Drury Lane in
1913, London audiences, though puzzled, were much more polite.

That year the company undertook a tour of South America. Diaghilev
decided to remain in Europe, leaving Baron Gunzbourg in charge. When
he waved farewell at Cherbourg little could Diaghilev have realized it was
the end of his relationship with Nijinsky.

The young Hungarian, Romola Pulska, who had first seen the Ballets
Russes in Budapest, was allowed to travel to South America with the
company, paying her own fare. It was during that voyage that Romola and

Nijinsky decided to marry. Diaghilev was in Venice when he learned the news. In *Two or Three Muses* Misia Sert relates that Diaghilev had invited her to play the score of *La Boutique Fantasque*:

> Performing elephantine capers across the room, in his enthusiasm he seized my parasol and opened it. I stopped playing with a start and told him to shut it, as it brought bad luck to open it indoors, and he was madly superstitious. Barely had I time to utter my warning when somebody knocked at the door. A telegram. . . .

It was, of course, the telegram announcing Nijinsky's marriage. 'Serge, overcome with a sort of hysteria, ready to go to any extreme, sobbing and shouting, gathered everyone around – Sert, Bakst, etc.' Perhaps one should treat Misia's account with some suspicion, Nevertheless, when Grigoriev saw Diaghilev again he was asked to sign the telegram to Nijinsky informing him of his dismissal from the company as the result of missing a performance in Rio de Janeiro. Curiously enough Grigoriev refused to be taken in by any sense of personal tragedy. He assumed that Diaghilev was relieved, in view of 'the failure of Nijinsky's last two ballets', and had decided that Nijinsky did not have it in him to become à great choreographer. After the break Nijinsky attempted to form a company to perform in London. When he asked Bakst to collaborate he learned that Diaghilev 'had declared war on him'. According to Romola, Bakst repeated Diaghilev's threat, 'As high as Nijinsky stands now, so low am I going to thrust him'.

In considering the future of the Ballets Russes one must also take into account the introduction of new, non-Russian elements. For *Le Dieu Bleu* Diaghilev had accepted a libretto by Cocteau and Frederigo Madrazo and music by Proust's friend Reynaldo Hahn – largely to satisfy the Paris *salons*. Also, Diaghilev was constantly seeking new oriental subjects for the public. As further evidence of the French infiltration there are the contributions of Debussy and Ravel to the 1912/13 seasons. Then, Diaghilev staged Florent Schmidt's *The Tragedy of Salome*, with a book by Robert d'Humieres. The year 1914 witnessed a broadening of this breach; Misia Sert's husband José-Maria became the first non-Russian designer to work for the company, while *The Legend of Joseph* had music by Richard Strauss and a book by Count Harry von Kessler and Hugo von Hofmannsthal.

Another prophetic sign was the introduction of the young Russian artist Natalia Gontcharova as the designer of Rimsky-Korsakov's *Le Coq d'Or*. The old 'family' was breaking up. Nijinsky had gone and in the 1914 season both Bakst and Benois played minor roles. Indeed, neither were to be used at all in the following two years, and Benois for not much longer. Fokine was persuaded to come back to the company; it took five hours of uninterrupted talk by Diaghilev to do it. Fokine insisted on being labelled not only *Choreographic Director* but *Premier Danseur*, and obtained an assurance that whilst he was in the company none of Nijinsky's ballets would be produced.

At this stage Diaghilev also suddenly revived the old 'Committee', of

Maria Kousnetzoff as Potiphar's wife in *La Légende de Joseph* 1914

OPPOSITE

Karsavina in *La Tragédie de Salomé*, designed by Soudeikine, 1913

OVERLEAF TOP

The young Léonid Massine in *La Légende de Joseph*, 1914, his first role with the Ballets Russes

OVERLEAF BELOW

Bakst's portrait of the young Massine, from the 1917 Programme. *Collection Léonid Massine*

PAGE 83

The cover of *Comœdia Illustré*, June 1912

80

whom only General Brezobrazov had died. His place was taken by Baron Gunzbourg. The programme planned for 1914 included Stravinsky's opera *Le Rossignol* and a minor piece devised by Bakst, *Midas*. The great problem facing Diaghilev was to find a dancer to play the youthful Joseph. It was solved when he found Massine in Moscow. Massine himself describes Diaghilev at that time as 'a creature from another world'. To give the reader an impression of Diaghilev's appearance at this period, one must quote Cocteau:

> (he) seemed to wear the smallest hat in creation. If you put on that hat, it would go down to your ears. For his head was so large that every hat was too small for him. His dancers called him Chinchilla because of an isolated white lock in his very dark dyed hair. He wore a tightly fitting fur coat and an opossum collar and at times he buttoned it up with safety pins. His face was a bull dog's, his smile a very young crocodile's, one tooth on the edge. To grind this tooth was for him a sign of pleasure, or fear, or anger. His mouth surmounted by a small moustache, he munched, seated in the back part of the loge, from where he watched his artists to whom he handed on no advice. And his wet eye looking downward had the curve of a Portuguese oyster. He conducted throughout the world a dance company, as confused and multicoloured as the fair of Nijni Novgorod. His one luxury was to discover a star.

He certainly discovered a new star – 'Rather provincial,' he told Grigoriev, 'but we'll soon put an end to that'. Massine never possessed Nijinsky's extraordinary gifts as a dancer but he was to prove a far more successful choreographer. Within one year he was the author of three new ballets – *Le Soleil de Nuit*, *Las Meninas* and *Kikimora*.

By this time war had been declared and Diaghilev found himself cut off not only from Russia but from many of his friends and most of his public. The 1914 season in Paris largely misfired, only *Le Coq d'Or* being well received. The London season which followed included opera as well as ballet, after which the company dispersed for holidays, due to reassemble in Berlin on 1 October. This meeting, of course, never took place. At the outbreak of war Diaghilev first settled in Switzerland, gathering around him a new 'Committee' – Bakst and Stravinsky, Gontcharova and her husband Larionov, Massine, and a new friend, the conductor Ernest Ansermet. He began to assemble the company, adding new dancers, Nelidova, Nemchinova, Spessivtseva, Idzikovski and Woizikovski. Unable to re-engage Fokine, Diaghilev had no alternative but to turn to Massine. Larionov became the boy's teacher, and indeed a major influence on Diaghilev himself. Massine was more successful than any of them had expected: 'You see,' said Diaghilev, 'Given the talent one can make a choreographer in no time.'

The war almost destroyed the Ballets Russes; the loss of the Paris and London seasons seemed insurmountable. Misia Sert urged Diaghilev to give up the struggle but in 1915 he signed a contract with the Metropolitan Opera for the Ballets Russes to makes its debut in New York – where Lydia

4ᵉ ANNÉE.— N° 17   1ᵉʳ JUIN 1912   NUMÉRO EXCEPTIONNEL de 60 PAGES. 8 HORS-TEXTES en COULEUR.   PRIX : 2 FRANC

Comœdia Illustré

Mᵐᵉ KARSAVINA et Mʳ BOLM dans THAMAR . △▽

richrome Comœdia Illustré   Costumes dessinés par Léon BAKST.

LARIONOW

LEFT

One of Bakst's costumes for *Papillons*
1914. *Collection Mark Birley, London*

ABOVE

Juan Gris' portrait drawing of Larionov,
for the 1921 Official Programme

PREVIOUS PAGE LEFT

Bakst's portrait of Nijinsky as the Faun,
from the cover of *Comœdia Illustré*, 15 May
1912. A version of the original drawing is
in the collection of the Wadsworth
Atheneum, Hartford, USA

PREVIOUS PAGE RIGHT

Bakst's costume design for the Blue God
from the 1912 Official Programme.
Versions of the original drawing are in the
collections of the Musée des Arts
Décoratifs, Paris, and Galleria del
Levante, Milan

OPPOSITE

TOP: Soudeikine's costume designs for *La
Tragédie de Salomé* 1913
BELOW: Fedorovsky's designs for the
opera *Khovantchina* 1913. Both from the
Souvenir Programme

Lopokova returned to the company. The American contract stipulated the participation of Nijinsky, then interned in Austria, but when he failed to arrive Massine danced the Faun, the first time anyone but its creator had appeared in the role. The American tour included sixteen different towns before a return to the Metropolitan on 3 April. Four days later Nijinsky arrived, suspicious, hostile and difficult.

Since the United States represented the only valuable wartime audience, Diaghilev negotiated another tour and had to agree to Nijinsky's directorship of the company. Before that they danced in Madrid in May, the beginning of a long and fruitful association with Spain. It was there that Massine created *Las Meninas* and became an expert in Spanish dancing. In due course, with Picasso's aid, this Spanish influence resulted in a series of famous ballets.

While Nijinsky directed the company in America, Diaghilev and a small group settled in Rome. In America Nijinsky composed a ballet to Richard Strauss's *Tyl Eulenspiegel*, but the season ended in chaos and the Diaghilev Ballet never appeared in America again. Rome, however, was to prove most productive. Diaghilev was surrounded by a brilliant group of friends – Picasso, Bakst, Cocteau, Balla, and the English composer Lord Berners. At the outbreak of the Russian Revolution he was giving a gala at the Costanzi Theatre, and in place of the Russian national anthem he had Stravinsky orchestrate *The Volga Boatmen*.

It was in Rome that Picasso met the ballerina Olga Koklova, whom he married. The partnership was short-lived and Olga was said to have followed Pablo round Paris with a loaded revolver, before declining into insanity.

RIGHT

Tchernicheva in Bakst's costume for *The Good Humoured Ladies*, 1917

FAR RIGHT

One of Bakst's costume designs for *The Good Humoured Ladies. Collection Evergreen House Foundation, Baltimore, USA*

In 1917 Massine created *The Good Humoured Ladies*, *Contes Russes*, and finally *Parade*, the first Diaghilev ballet designed by Picasso. The title of the ballet derived from the costume for the character, The American Manager, a cardboard skyscraper with a sign reading PARADE. Diaghilev accepted all of Cocteau's innovations, only stopping short of the Managers delivering lines through megaphones. He refused to allow the spoken word in a ballet.

Guillaume Apollinaire claimed that in *Parade*:

Picasso the cubist painter and Leonide Massine, the boldest of choreographers, have given cubism concrete form, and achieved the first union of painting and dancing, modelling and mime, which is to herald a fuller art . . . for hitherto decoration and choreography have only been linked by superficial means. . . .

That seems a bit hard on the Fokine-Bakst partnership which was equally, if not more successful, and as influential. But as Lifar points out, although the ballet was an undoubted success in Paris, it was, in fact, 'a far cry from the wild enthusiasm with which his early ballets had been greeted'.

Picasso's curtain for *Parade*, 1917, reproduced from the Official Programme. Original design, Musée National d'Art Moderne, Paris

OPPOSITE TOP

Picasso's drawing of a group of Russian dancers *c*. 1919, showing his wife Olga Kokhlova in the foreground. *Collection Picasso Estate*

OPPOSITE BELOW

Dancers wearing Picasso's costumes for *Parade*

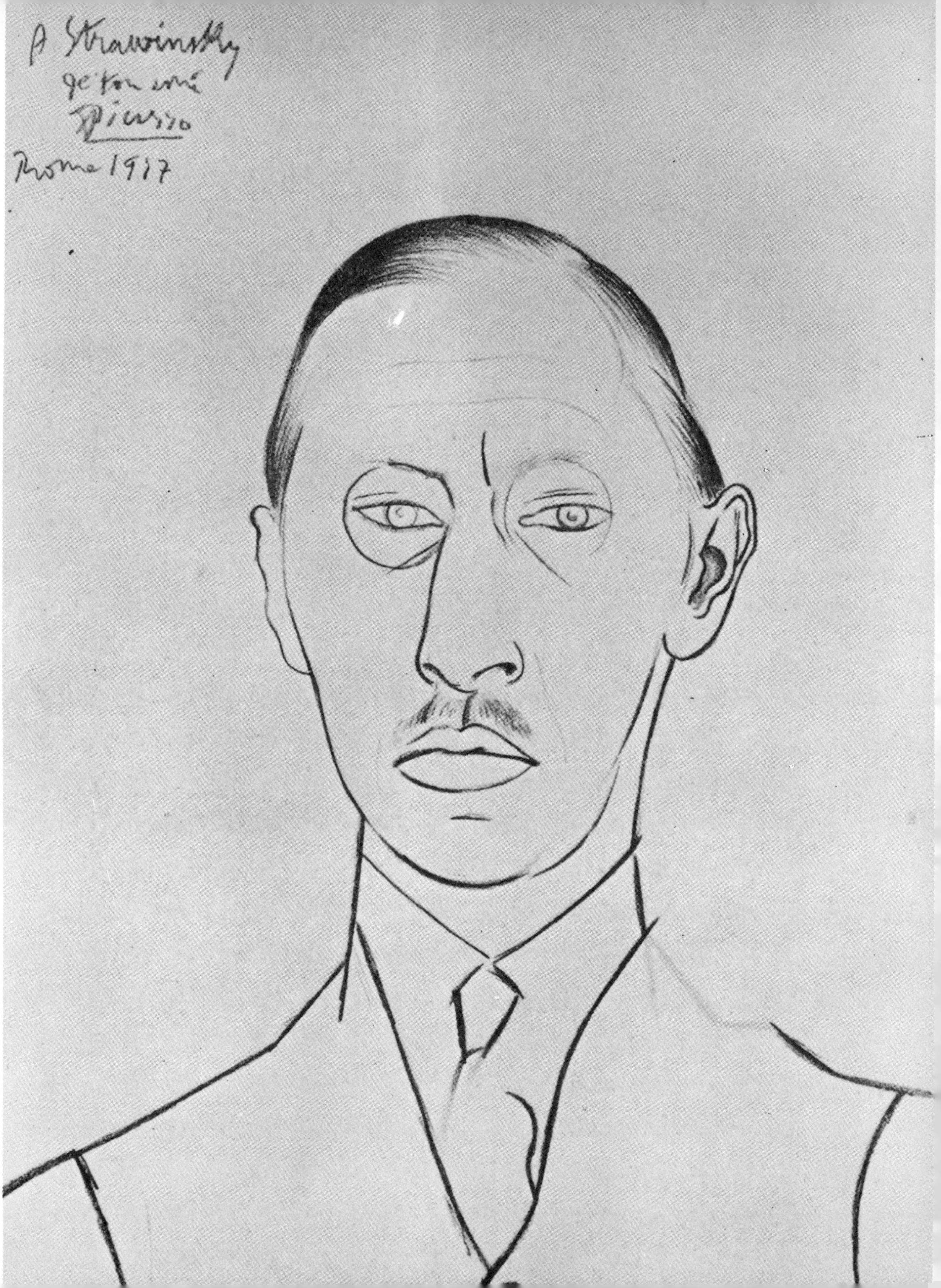
A Stravinsky
de son ami
Picasso
Roma 1917

Jean Cocteau, who had been associated with Diaghilev since the first season in 1909, and had produced the now famous posters for *Le Spectre de la Rose*, was ambitious to be the author of a successful ballet. He tells of a conversation one night in 1912 in the Place de la Concorde:

> We were coming home for supper after the performance. Nijinsky was sulking as usual. He was walking ahead of us. Diaghilev was amused at my behaviour. When I questioned him on his reserve, he stopped, adjusted his monocle and said to me – 'Surprise me' . . . In 1917, the evening of the premier of *Parade*, I surprised him.

With *Parade*, Diaghilev and the Ballets Russes entered its last phase. The first period united Fokine's talents, oriental spectacle and the decor of Leon Bakst; the second introduced Stravinsky and the choreography of Nijinsky, and younger Russian designers like Gontcharova and Larionov; the final period shows the virtual discarding of the Russianness of the company, even to the recruitment of foreign dancers, among them, Sokolova, Ninette de Valois, Markova and Anton Dolin (albeit only English ones). Diaghilev's discarding of old friends, and old-fashioned artists, was noted by many. Massine writes: 'I had long ago realised that Diaghilev was ruthless in anything that affected the work of the company . . . he often told me that in the theatre there were no friends. . . .'

Romola Nijinsky, smarting under Diaghilev's treatment of her husband, concluded:

> . . . He made Bakst and dropped Roerich and Benois for him. He raised Stravinsky and played him off against Prokofiev. He launched Massine and changed him for Dolin, Lifar and others. And thus Bakst was cast away for Larionov. Diaghilev did not keep his artists with him, giving chances to all of them. Once they were discovered and developed he threw them away as used gloves. . . .

All this tends to confirm Nabokov's assessment that for the purposes of the ballet, Diaghilev's friends and associates were seen by him as objects to be used, to be discarded.

It must however be understood that Diaghilev's break with Russianism and his experimentation with new art forms were partly of necessity and partly a search for novelties. The break with Fokine and Nijinsky also meant a break with Russian tradition; the war and the revolution further contributed to a search for broader source material; and if the company was to continue as an artistic and commercial force it had to introduce new works, reflecting the new post-war atmosphere.

As always in Diaghilev's career a particular individual acted as cipher and mentor; in this case it was Cocteau. His influence can be traced back to 1912

when he helped devise *Le Dieu Bleu*. It is no coincidence that at that time Diaghilev began to use other French material, the music of Hahn, Ravel, Debussy, and the designs of Sert. As early as 1914 Cocteau suggested a ballet based on the circus, which he wished to design himself. He seized on the advent of Massine, a new, unformed choreographer, receptive to his ideas, to further influence Diaghilev.

As Douglas Cooper writes: 'Diaghilev dominated the artistic life of his Ballets Russes entirely so that his approval had to be secured for any ballet project which he himself had not originated.'

Picasso's contributions in the following years, all to Massine ballets, included *The Three Cornered Hat, Pulcinella* and *Cuadro Flamenco*. Long periods in Spain, partly due to the enthusiasm of King Alfonso, are reflected in these works, as is Massine's expertise in Spanish dancing and the music of the composer de Falla, who was to become a regular collaborator in modern ballet.

In 1917 the company embarked on a second tour of South America in which Nijinsky again appeared, now seriously unhinged. On 26 September 1917, in Buenos Aires, he danced for the last time in a theatre.

OPPOSITE TOP

Picasso's curtain for *Le Tricorne*, from the 1919–1920 Programme. *Now in the collection of the Seagram Building, New York*

OPPOSITE BELOW

Dancers rehearsing *Le Tricorne* in London 1919, a sketch by Picasso. *Collection Picasso Estate*

ABOVE

Bakst's caricature of Picasso from the 1917 programme, probably done in Rome during preparations for *Parade*

ABOVE RIGHT

Picasso's self-portrait reproduced in the Official Programme for the 1919–1920 Season

Despite the artistic renewal and new creativity within the company in the last years of the war, financially things were going from bad to worse. When it looked as though the company might be disbanded, a new friend came to the rescue, Coco Chanel, placing a large sum at Diaghilev's disposal.

In the end Diaghilev was forced to accept an invitation to appear in a music-hall bill at the Coliseum in London in September 1918. The company danced alongside Jack Lane – 'Yorkshire rustic comedian' – and a troupe of performing apes. Nevertheless the splendour of *Cleopatra*, in Delaunay's new setting, and Massine's lively *Good Humoured Ladies* soon eliminated any sense of incongruity. The company stayed for six months, at last enjoying an orderly and peaceful existence. The programme was changed every Monday and Thursday so that London enjoyed a large repertoire of old and new ballets. In *Laughter in the Next Room* Osbert Sitwell records the joy of finding the Russian Ballet in London at the end of the war. He had been one of its great enthusiasts during the seasons of 1912, 1913, 1914:

That one would ever see the ballet again then seemed a hope beyond ambition; nor afterwards when I had come back to England was there any sign that the company would ever reappear in London. For years little news of it had reached England, and none of its most faithful followers could say where it was. Therefore its return in September 1918 possessed for my brother and myself all the force of a portent.

Sitwell noted the new Spanish tang to the repertoire and especially admired the wit of Lopokova and Massine.

The pleasant existence in London was shattered by a fortnight's notice from Oswald Stoll. Fortunately the Alhambra Theatre became free and Stoll agreed to the company transferring there, after a visit to Manchester. Back in London Diaghilev presented two new ballets, *La Boutique Fantasque* and *The Three-Cornered Hat*. So successful was this second season that in September 1919 the company were back again at the Empire Theatre, this time presenting *Parade* which Osbert Sitwell found 'the most tragic and

96

OPPOSITE

Derain's setting for *La Boutique Fantasque*, 1919, from the Official Programme

ABOVE

Karsavina and Massine in *La Boutique Fantasque*

ABOVE RIGHT

Picasso's portrait of André Derain, for the Official Programme 1919–1920

RIGHT

Dancers in *La Boutique Fantasque*

most original of the newer spectacles'. A string of royal visitors enhanced the season – King George V, the Shah of Persia on a State Visit, and even the company's old friend, Alfonso of Spain.

The return of Stravinsky marked 1920; he and Diaghilev had been on unfriendly terms since 1916, although Diaghilev used his early composition *Fireworks*. On one occasion Diaghilev commented: 'Our success has gone to his head'. Their quarrel was over the not unusual subject of money – Diaghilev owing Stravinsky 30,000 francs. 'Together with success' says Misia Sert, 'Stravinsky developed a taste for money'. As the gulf grew between them, Stravinsky began to be more interested in America. Eventually he announced that his 'religious convictions did not allow him to apply his art to anything as base as ballet'. Diaghilev retorted, 'I hear that Stravinsky, my first son, is dedicating himself to the dual worship of God and Mammon'. Now, the reunion resulted in the ballet *Le Chant du Rossignol*, based on an earlier Stravinsky opera, with charming designs by the great painter Matisse. Stravinsky also adapted the music of Pergolesi for *Pulcinella* and there was a new version by Massine of *The Rite of Spring*.

It was at this time that relations between Diaghilev and Massine began to deteriorate; Massine wished to have himself designated as *Maître de Ballet* on the programmes, to which Diaghilev replied that he must compose ten ballets to be so honoured. The final break came in Rome early in 1921 and for a second time Grigoriev was the messenger of doom.

After a tour of Paris, Rome and Madrid the Ballet returned to London to the rebuilt Princes Theatre, then under the direction of Charles B. Cochran, who was a great admirer. Cochran proposed that Diaghilev be appointed 'International Minister of Arts', believing that the

> wonderful combination of artistry, talent and beauty (of the Russian Ballet) has done more to improve the taste of the world in colour and music than any institution ever founded. Its influence has extended far beyond the Theatre.

In London Diaghilev was impressed with the success of *Chu Chin Chow* then in its third year at Her Majesty's Theatre. If this popular musical could seemingly run forever, he mused, why not a ballet. Seized with the idea of re-mounting Petipa's *La Belle au Bois Dormant* he persuaded Oswald Stoll to finance the production. The contract, however, stipulated that the cost must be repaid from box office takings. On signing this portentious document Diaghilev made the sign of the cross and sighed, 'What will be, will be'. So deeply Russian a subject (albeit of French origin), required one of Diaghilev's old Russian friends as designer. Benois was not available, so he had to go cap in hand to Bakst. Since the debacle of *La Boutique Fantasque* they had not spoken. Bakst in fact was a sick man and the prospect of five sets and more than one hundred costumes was frightening. After a series of productions for Ida Rubinstein he longed to return to the Ballets Russes – but not before he extracted from Diaghilev a contract as tough as Oswald Stoll's. The programme referred to 'The entire production by M. Leon Bakst', and furthermore Diaghilev had to promise that Bakst would also design Stravinsky's new opera *Mavra* (a promise he characteristically refused to keep).

The original production of *The Sleeping Princess* in 1890, with its lavish decor and magnificent choreography was the crowning glory of the Russian Imperial Ballet. Re-staging it was an audacious undertaking. The company had to literally re-learn pure classic dancing, and Diaghilev engaged as soloists many of the former stars of the Imperial Theatre – Spessivtseva, Trefilova, Egorova, Schollar, Vladimirov, Vilzak. As a nostalgic gesture, Carlotta Brianza, the original Aurora, was now given the role of Carabosse, while Cecchetti, the original Bluebird, danced at the hundredth performance. For the choreography Diaghilev engaged Sergeyev, the former regisseur of the Maryinsky Theatre, and called in Bronislava Nijinska for new numbers. (Nijinska was to become the company's new choreographer, and one of its greatest.) He added themes from *Casse-Noisette*, and asked Stravinsky to re-orchestrate part of Tchaikovsky's original score.

Preparations for this great event appeared to give Diaghilev new life. 'I was reminded of his activity in 1909, when preparing his very first season in

OPPOSITE TOP

The arrival of Carrabosse in *La Belle au Bois Dormant* (The Sleeping Beauty) at the Alhambra Theatre, London, 1921

OPPOSITE BELOW

Enrico Cecchetti in old age, lithograph by Randolph Schwabe

R. Schwabe

Paris', comments Grigoriev. But the problems seemed almost insurmountable. Diaghilev later described the dress rehearsal as a disaster:

> The stage machinery did not work; the trees in the enchanted wood did not sprout; the backdrop shifts did not come off; the tulle skirts got tangled in the flats. The premier suffered accordingly, and the financial losses that ensued were incalculable. By staging this ballet I very nearly killed off my theatrical ventures abroad.

He concluded that it was not his business to concern himself 'with reviving the triumphs of days gone by'.

The production was given for one hundred and fifteen performances at The Alhambra. Bakst made a valiant effort, but although the Bibiena sets were superb architectural evocations, and the costumes sumptuous creations in the French manner, the total image was pastiche.

Arnold Haskell found the production almost too scholarly for popular appeal:

> To discuss it over a dinner table had needed a real knowledge of dancing, and the usual descriptive adjectives for the latest music and decor were meaningless here . . . it gave the ballet public rigid standards, and today in

TIL EULENSPIEGEL
CHÂTELAINE

ABOVE

Erté's design for Prince Charming in *The Sleeping Beauty*, a maquette done at Diaghilev's request in 1922

ABOVE RIGHT

Lydia Lopokova in 1921

PRECEDING PAGES

Top: One of Picasso's variations for the setting of *Le Tricorne* 1919
Below left: Picasso's final set for *Pulchinella* 1920.
Both private collections

Right: Costume design by Robert E. Jones for *Tyl Eulenspiegel*, 1916 *collection Philip Dyer, London*

OPPOSITE

Setting for *Le Astuzie Femminili* by José-Maria Sert, from the 1920 programme

England its influence in retrospect is tremendous. No one who saw those performances could ever think the same about dancing again. This seemingly light entertainment was one of Diaghilev's most profound lessons in ballet and stage craft.

The brave venture ended disastrously. When the production closed in London Oswald Stoll sequestered all the properties until the remaining cost was paid. Stoll had advanced £20,000 of which less than half had been recovered. Anxious to honour the centenary of Petipa's birth in 1922, Diaghilev arranged part of the ballet as *Le Mariage d'Aurore*. He used Benois' decor from *Le Pavillon d'Armide* and in his search for new costumes approached the Russian designer Erté, then living in Monte Carlo. Some designs exist, but Erté was not able to undertake the commission, which was eventually given to Gontcharova. Princesse Edmund de Polignac once more came to Diaghilev's rescue.

The remaining seven years of Diaghilev's life have been described by his biographer Arnold Haskell, as 'in search of lost youth'. The period opened with new works *Le Renard* and *Les Noces*, designed by Larionov and Gontcharova, choreographed by Nijinska – the first all-Russian team for

BALLETS RUSSES

years on a major work.

This period of artistic renewal was facilitated by an agreement with the Opera House at Monte Carlo whereby the company became known as 'Les Ballets Russes de Monte Carlo, direction Serge de Diaghilev'. The ballet thus had a permanent home, and facilities for rehearsal. They stayed at Monte Carlo for six months each year so that, after holidays, four months remained for touring.

It was at Monte Carlo in 1923 that some new recruits arrived from Russia, former pupils of Nijinska; the least gifted seemed to be a boy named Serge Lifar, destined to become the new favourite and an international star. Lifar recalls:

In a small group of people walking towards us I made out a man in a fur overcoat, a soft hat on his head. He seemed a giant to me. He came forward swinging his walking-stick. A Russian *barin* of a past age. In his rather fleshy face, under white locks reminding me of a St Bernard dog, shone two friendly brown eyes, eyes that expressed at one and the same time vivacity, mildness and a kind of sadness. It was Diaghilev. One could not doubt that for an instant. He was art incarnate. A man with the

Felia Doubrovska in *Les Noces*, 1923

power to change life, to transmute reality. The inventor, the man we dreamed of having as master.

The 1923 season at the Gaieté Lyrique was memorable for Nijinska's *Les Noces*, fulfilling the choreographic promise once expected of her brother, and giving the world one of the few undisputed masterpieces of modern ballet. Gerald and Sara Murphy, friends of Scott Fitzgerald (models for his book *Tender is the Night*), gave a celebratory party after the ballet, attended by Picasso, Milhaud, Cocteau, Tristan Tzara, novelist Blaise Cendrars, and the Ballet's principals – they were told not to invite the corps de ballet as Diaghilev would not have approved.

Gerald Murphy was taking painting lessons from· Gontcharova and attached himself to the Ballets Russes. He found:

> In addition to being the focal centre of the whole modern movement in the arts, the Diaghilev ballet was a kind of movement in itself. Anybody who was interested in the company became a member automatically. You knew everybody, you knew all the dancers and everybody asked your opinion on things.

Later Murphy himself designed Cole Porter's *Within the Quota* for the

Ballets Suédois.

In the following year there was a marked absence of anything Russian in the programme, unless one accepts the Slavophiling of English names. An English dancer who had performed in *The Sleeping Princess* in London, now re-joined the ballet; Diaghilev called him Patrikeyev – his real name was Sydney Francis Patrick Chippendale Healey-Kay, a mouthful for anyone, let alone a Russian who had never mastered English. That was soon changed and Anton Dolin achieved fame in the revival of *Daphnis and Cloe*. Another English addition to the company was Ninette de Valois.

The last years of Diaghilev were marked by a remarkable creativity, but the majority of the new works were of only passing interest. Diaghilev virtually abandoned the typically Russian narrative ballet for divertissements, in which any serious artistic quality, or experimentation, lay in the music or decor. He renewed his collaboration with Stravinsky, followed by a series of Prokofiev ballets; and employed such outstanding artists as de Chirico, Gabo and Pevsner, Rouault, Tchelitchew, and the French naïf painter, Bauchant.

It was also a period of constant financial worry, which in turn led to

OPPOSITE TOP

Marie Laurencin's curtain design for *Les Biches*, 1924, from the Official Programme

OPPOSITE BELOW

Portrait of Serge Prokofiev by Natalia Gontcharova. *Private collection*

ABOVE LEFT

Nikitina in *Les Biches* 1924, bronze statuette by the Hungarian sculptor Strobl. *Private collection. Photograph courtesy Sotheby's*

ABOVE RIGHT

Nemchinova and Vilzak in *Les Biches*, 1924

defections and the search for new dancers and choreographers, as well as numerous compromises for the sake of patronage and engagements. During one of these economic crises Diaghilev suddenly announced his intention to sell Picasso's curtain for *Le Tricorne* and the decor for *Cuadro Flamenco*. For these reasons, perhaps, plus a lowering of vitality as he grew older, and also ill-health through diabetes, Diaghilev appeared to lose interest in ballet. Rare books became a new passion. In the early days he 'operated' through the choreographers – Fokine, Nijinsky, Massine, who either shared his ideas, or accepted them. This did not apply to Nijinska who was altogether too original and independent, or to Balanchine, her successor, who arrived from Russia 'fully formed' so to speak.

The 1924 season was again dominated by Nijinska – *Les Biches* with its charming decor by Marie Laurencin, *Les Fâcheux*, designed by Braque, Mussorgsky's *Night on the Bare Mountain*, and especially *Le Train Bleu*, set on the Côte d'Azur, in which the young Anton Dolin shone – much to Lifar's chagrin. Cocteau was once again responsible for the scenario, and the beach costumes were by Chanel. The decor by the sculptor Henri Laurens proved dull, which prompted Diaghilev to ask Picasso for the famous act-drop – of two cavorting giantesses – to enliven the overture (to music by Milhaud). Cocteau was inspired by seeing Dolin perform gymnastic exercises backstage. As a result the ballet typifies the new style of elaborate, often daring, acrobatics which characterizes so much modern ballet.

Diaghilev also tried his hand again at opera, aroused by a new admiration for Gounod. The result was *Le Médicin Malgré Lui*, and *Philémon et Baucis*, both designed by Benois, now back from Russia. They represent the last collaboration between the two old friends. 'Diaghilev no longer likes my decors' commented Benois, who on seeing the new productions found himself 'highly embarrassed':

I could not remain indifferent to what was fascinating and alluring – in

other words to the talent displayed – but that only added to my embarrass-
ment. I was well acquainted with Diaghilev's inclination towards
extremes, an inclination that encouraged him to indulge in his favourite
'pamps'. . . . The search for novelty and the wish to keep pace with the
century had led Seriozha, our 'aristocrat' Seriozha, so far as to present on
the stage of the Opera an apotheosis of the Soviet regime. . . .

(Benois is here referring to a Soviet Constructivist ballet of 1927.) Reviewing the Russian Ballet's progress in 1925, André Levinson found

. . . it is harder than ever to surmise the exact policy of the company's
management. The Ballets Russes' theory and practice have altered twice
in three years . . . Fokine's departure in 1912 provoked a crisis which
Diaghilev has not yet succeeded in solving . . . The question 'What to do
next?' is still as urgent as ever.

Diaghilev was anxious to return to London, always the scene of artistic
and financial success; the large debt to Stoll seemed immovable. Eventually
Stoll offered the Coliseum for a series of seasons, so that the debt could be
paid off. 1924 proved a momentous year. Nijinska resigned – largely out of
resentment against the new protégé, Lifar. Then a new batch of recruits

from Russia arrived, including Alexandra Danilova and Georges Balan-chivadze, later to win fame as Georges Balanchine. There was yet another addition to the company, the fourteen-year-old Alice Marks, renamed Alicia Markova. It was also in London, on 28 December, that Diaghilev learned of the death of one of his oldest friends, and greatest collaborators, Leon Bakst. They had not spoken for years.

Being without a choreographer, Diaghilev then re-engaged Massine, but he too, in time, would give way to Balanchine. The latter, meanwhile, was given an opportunity to show his mettle on opera productions at Monte Carlo. Then, in 1925 Diaghilev entrusted him with a new production of Stravinsky's *Le Chant du Rossignol*, followed by his first original work, *Barabau*, for which a sketch by Utrillo was used as decor. Meanwhile Massine, back after five years, produced *Zéphyre et Flore* and *Les Matelots*. The first had a charming decor by Braque; the second introduced a new artist to the company, Pruna. In both Lifar rose as a star – which, as Haskell points out, in Diaghilev's life means 'the setting of a former one'. In this case it was Dolin, who then left the company (later to return, it must be added).

The appearances in London resulted in the final re-payment to Stoll. Diaghilev was now free to negotiate independent British seasons. He found a new friend and backer in Lord Rothermere. One immediate result was an interest in English themes: Constant Lambert was commissioned to produce a score for *Romeo and Juliet* and Lord Berners for *The Triumph of Neptune*. Nijinska was recalled for the Shakespeare ballet. Diaghilev decided no decor was required, since Shakespeare never used any; the company wore simple costumes, only the principals in period dress. To add to the hotch-potch, the back-drops by painters Max Ernst and Joán Miró bore no relationship to the subject. Not unaptly the ballet was termed 'a rehearsal in two parts with no decor'. Its presentation in Paris on 18 May provided the Surrealists with the excuse for a demonstration against Ernst and Miró for collaborating with 'capitalists', showering the audience with leaflets signed by Louis Aragon and André Breton. It proved Diaghilev's most enlivening first-night since the debacle over *Le Sacre du Printemps*.

All the other new works in 1926 were by Balanchine. *La Pastorale* had two main characters, Film Star and Telegraph Boy – Lifar complete with bicycle. *Jack in the Box*, his second novelty, music by Satie, decor by Derain, also failed to make an impression. *The Triumph of Neptune*, performed at the second London season of 1926, was a great success. The scenario was by Sacheverell Sitwell, with decor based on Victorian prints. Balanchine was acclaimed both for his choreography and for his dancing of the drunken negro. These seasons delighted Diaghilev because of their financial success. At the first he introduced to London new ballets such as *Parade* and *Les Noces*, and a Satie Festival. At the second he revived former favourites, *Swan Lake*, *L'Oiseau de Feu*, and *L'Après-midi d'un Faune*, now danced by Lifar.

The 'Soviet' ballet to which Benois objected was *Le Pas d'Acier*, with music by Prokofiev and designs by the Russian painter Yakoulov. Its depiction of contemporary Russian life caused some stir, but the work was never successful. In contrast Balanchine's *La Chatte* must be regarded as his first masterpiece, enhanced with a plastic Constructivist set by Gabo and Pevsner. These two works, with their involvement in Russian contemporary art, showed Diaghilev's nostalgia for his homeland. To some extent this was aroused by his friendship with Prokofiev; indeed he expressed a desire to visit Soviet Russia, but feared he might not be able to return. At one stage Diaghilev declared that Constructivism in painting was dead, 'but it is still very much alive in music . . . as well as choreography'. (It was one of his many misjudgments of modern art. Russian Constructivism has

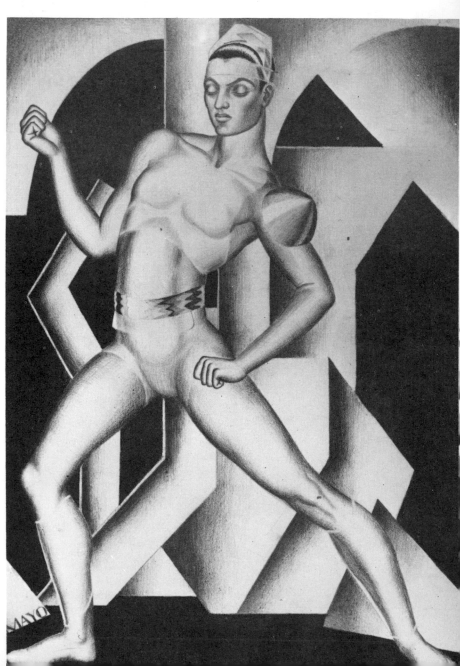

Portrait of Serge Lifar in *La Chatte*, 1927, by Mayo. *Collection Philip Dyer, London*

A scene from *Ode* 1928, designed by Tchelitchew

emerged as one of the most important collective art experiments of the century, and its exponents are increasingly highly rated, both critically and in the sale rooms.)

In 1927 Diaghilev also staged a concert version of Stravinsky's opera *Œdipus Rex* – which proved unsuccessful; in 1928 he introduced the Russian composer, Nabokov, and another Russian designer, Tchelitchew, in Massine's *Ode*. This last was devised by Boris Kochno, who in 1921 had become Diaghilev's secretary. He was to exert considerable influence in the last period of the Ballets Russes. Arnold Haskell describes Kochno as a necessary 'intermediary' with youth and new ideas:

. . . It is for this reason that during the final years Kochno possessed almost a greater influence over him than anyone had in his whole career. It was not that Diaghilev accepted every project without criticism, but he allowed himself to be influenced, often against his own better judgment, because he felt that in the long run youth must be right. He began to suspect his own judgments as well as those of people of his own generation, and often he hated the results though he was loath to admit it. Kochno as well as librettist became his absolute adviser in decor, costumes, choreography and even music.

Since Diaghilev's death, Kochno and Serge Lifar have proved his most loyal disciples, keeping alive the memory of his achievement in numerous books and exhibitions.

The year 1927 marked the twentieth anniversary of Diaghilev's presentations in Paris. A special season opened at the Sarah Bernhardt Theatre on 27 May, and Stravinsky came to conduct *L'Oiseau de Feu* and *Œdipus Rex*. Diaghilev, who was now fifty-five, got wind of a special party or presentation from the company. He assembled them on the stage, saying,

> It has come to my knowledge that you intend celebrating my twentieth season in Paris. I am deeply grateful to you for the thought, but I implore you not to act on it. . . . I abhor jubilees in general and my own in particular. A jubilee is the beginning of an end; something that rounds off a career. I am not ready to give up. I wish to continue working. . . . I wish to remain always young. . . .

The celebratory year was continued in a vast London programme, which included twenty-two revivals, as well as the new ballets and a Stravinsky Festival. By this time Diaghilev was bored with the continued success of old favourites like *Cleopatra* and *Schéhérazade* – his 'youthful peccadillos', as he called them – which still broke box office records.

In the following year Balanchine produced his great work *Apollon Musagète*, conducted by the composer Stravinsky, with an enchanting decor by Bauchant. The work also provided a star role for Lifar. Diaghilev was delighted with the new ballet; he described the music as one of Stravinsky's 'masterpieces, the product of true artistic maturity'. Balanchine's choreography, he felt, 'fits it perfectly, classical in style, treated from the modern aspect'.

Another London season was threatened by the withdrawal of Lord Rothermere's support, but with the help of Sir Thomas Beecham His Majesty's Theatre was made available. There Beecham's arrangement of music by Handel was played for Balanchine's *The Gods Go A-Begging*, so hurriedly staged that Bakst's old decor for *Daphnis and Chloe* and costumes from *Les Tentations de la Bergère* were used. Despite this it proved popular.

The year ended on a nostalgic note. On 27 December Nijinsky came to the Paris Opera to see a performance of *Petrushka*, in which his former partner Karsavina was appearing. There was a hope that the ballet might repair his mental instability, but he remained as disturbed as ever. At the New Year's Eve Party, a few days later, Diaghilev wistfully pointed out to Grigoriev that of all his old friends in the creation of the Ballets Russes only he, Grigoriev and Walter Nouvel remained with him. Serge Lifar noted his growing lack of interest. In his diary for 4 February 1929, he recorded:

> I am certain that this will be the last season of Diaghilev's Ballets. Serguei Pavlovitch is at breaking point. His interest in ballet is continually waning . . . The discovery of some old book means more to him than a creation. Our family is breaking up. . . .

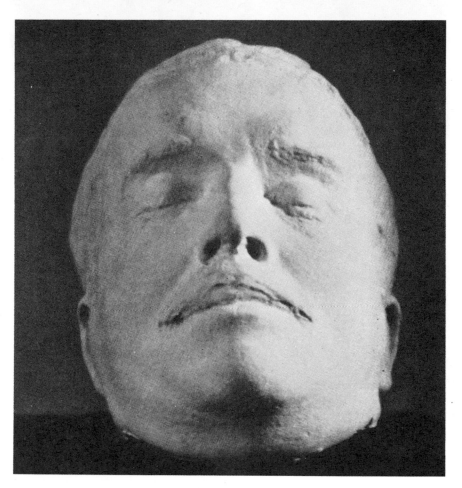

THEODORE KOSLOF

With Balanchine's supremacy Massine left the company for the last time.
In 1929 Lifar was given his first choreographic opportunity in a new production of *Renard*, but the great achievement of the year was Balanchine's *The
Prodigal Son*. This famous work, to the music of Prokofiev, with decor by
Rouault, was received with great enthusiasm. So, too, was a second
Balanchine ballet *Le Bal* with de Chirico's designs, for which Dolin
returned to the company. He also assumed the mantle of Nijinsky in a
revival of *Le Spectre de la Rose*. When Diaghilev spoke to the company after
its last performance in London on 26 July he looked pale and feverish: 'We
have a busy year before us. All my contracts are signed; and for the first time
in my whole career we have an uninterrupted series of engagements already
fixed.'

Like so many Russians Diaghilev was immensely superstitious. He never
forgot that a fortune teller had foreseen that he would die on water – hence
his hatred of boats. He was seriously ill throughout the last London season
in 1929. When Walter Nouvel met him at the station in Paris he was shocked:

He was years older and dragged his feet as he walked. From the hotel he
telephoned his doctor who came immediately. After the consultation I

found him sunk in a chair. The doctor had just told him that he had had a very narrow escape in London, that it was essential for him to give up his immediate plans, his Venetian holiday, in order to go to Vichy.

Diaghilev ignored this advice. The Ballet had a week's engagement at Vichy from 4 August. He then went on to the Salzburg Festival with the composer Markevich, his latest protégé, visited Hindemith, and spent time searching for books. After ten days he journeyed on to Venice alone. He was joined in Venice on 9 August by Lifar, who hardly recognized him. After 12 August Diaghilev never again rose from his bed.

Boris Kochno was summoned to Venice. Coco Chanel and Misia Sert were also visiting the city. On 19 August at 5.45 a.m. his breathing ceased. The doctor announced 'it is the end'.

In her biography Misia Sert relates:

An essentially Russian manifestation, such as you meet in Dostoievsky's characters, took place in that little hotel room, where the greatest magician in the world of art had come to die. Serge's death must have been the spark that caused the explosion of the mutual hatred pent up between the two boys who had lived so close to him. A kind of roar struck the silence with authentic drama. Kochno hurled himself on Lifar, who was kneeling at the other side of the bed. They rolled on the floor tearing at each other, biting one another like the savage beasts. They were in the grip of real fury. Two mad dogs were fighting over the body of their master.

The funeral took place two days later. A gondola draped in black and gold carried Diaghilev's body to the island of San Michele where he is buried. His attendants included Misia Sert, Coco Chanel, Baroness Catherine d'Erlanger, Boris Kochno and Serge Lifar.

6 DIAGHILEV'S HERITAGE

Diaghilev's bequest to the World of Ballet, after 20 years' creative endeavour, and to the public in general, is manifold; he created or inspired some of the most perfect theatrical works of art, and handed to future generations a number of imperishable masterpieces. *Ballet for All* (1970) lists thirteen of his ballets still regularly performed all over the world, quite apart from themes or musical scores used by the Ballets Russes which are constantly re-interpreted. After his death his closest collaborators – dancers, choreographers, composers, designers – continued to contribute to and influence every theatrical (and indeed cinematic) form of entertainment. Above all his permanent memorial is the establishment of classical and experimental dance as a lively art form, capable of expressing the widest range of human experience and emotion, in an international formula unheeded by the barrier of language.

It has already been pointed out that Diaghilev was not the instigator of this internationalism; nor was he the first to bring Russian dance to the West. The paradoxical history of Russian ballet reveals the immense importance of foreign dancers and choreographers, including the great Petipa, in forming a tradition associated with the Imperial Maryinsky company; which in turn became the styles of both the Ballets Russes and the Soviet companies. Before Diaghilev organized his first season, Lydia Kyasht brought Russian ballet to the London stage, with Karsavina and Pavlova also acting as heralds of the new Russian tradition.

LEFT

Karsavina in J. M. Barrie's play *The Truth About the Russian Dancers*, 1922, designed by Paul Nash. *Photograph courtesy John Carr Doughty*

SEPTEMBER 14th, 1908.

EMPIRE
PROGR
Subject to alteration at the dis

	OVERTURE ... "La Sirène" ... ... *Auber.*
1	Harry Lamore.
2	Johnny & Charlie.
3	The Empire Ladies' Quartette.

4 COPPÉLIA.

A BALLET IN TWO SCENES BY CH. NUITTER AND A. SAINT LEON.

Produced and Dances arranged, by ALEXANDER GENÉE

Music by LEO DELIBES.

Scenery by JOSEPH HARKER.

Costumes designed and supervised by C. WILHELM.

The Dresses executed by Miss HASTINGS and MORRIS ANGEL & SONS.   Machinist, W. SHELDON.
Properties by P. GRIEVESON.   Electrician, C. WINTER.   Wigs by CLARKSON.

SWANILDA (a Village Girl) .... **Mlle. LYDIA KYAKSHT**
FRANZ (her Sweetheart) .... Mme. ZANFRETTA
COPPÉLIUS (an Eccentric Inventor of Mechanical Figures) ....Mr. FRED FARREN
IRMA (the Betrothed of Laszlo) .... Miss E. CLERC
COPPÉLIA (a Doll, Coppelius's Masterpiece) .... Miss E. COLLIER
LASZLO (a Slovak Pedlar) .... Mr. B. FORD
The Burgomaster and his Wife ....Mr. JAMESON and Miss M. PASTON
Innkeeper... .... Miss SHEPHERD
FRIENDS OF SWANILDA .... { Misses BANKS, BOSETTI, HILL, PETERS, PAVER ARRIGONI, OSMOND, and RUSHTON
CZARDAS and MAZURKA { Misses TREVESICK, DAWSON, KAYGILL,
DANCERS, VILLAGERS, { EDWARDES, ROULLRIGHT, LYONS, B. COLLIER,
MUSICIANS, &c. { L. PIACENTINI, B. ARIGONI, E. McFARLANE, and the Ladies and Gentlemen of the Corps-de-Ballet.

Scene I.—A VILLAGE ON THE BORDERS OF GALICIA.

VALSE................. ....… .... **Mlle. LYDIA KYAKSHT**
MAZURKA................... ....THE CORPS DE BALLET
PAS COMIQUE (Slovak) .... Miss E. CLERC and Mr. B. FORD
GRAND BALLET (Slav Theme, with Variations) { **Mlle. LYDIA KYAKSHT**, Misses PAVER, PETERS, B. HILL, L. OSMOND, and BOSETTI
CZARDAS (Hungarian National Dance)........ { Mme. ZANFRETTA, Miss E. CLERC, Mr. FORD, and CORPS DE BALLET.

The scene opens with Swanilda, on the morning of the Burgomaster's golden wedding, discovering a life-like doll in the window of Coppelius' house ; as she gazes at it her lover Franz kisses his hand to the mechanical figure, Swanilda becomes jealous under the impression that the doll is a living girl ; the doll-maker issues from his house and is seized upon by a crowd of students headed by Franz ; he drives them off, but in his excitement drops his door key ; this is picked up by a friend of Swanilda, and she and her maidens determine to explore the mysterious workshop. Prior to doing so the Burgomaster and his wife arrive, and are treated to a Czardas by a Slovak Pedlar and Irma, while Swanilda puts her lover to the test of an Ear of Corn, accompanied by a Valse on Hungarian Themes.

During the Entr'acte of Three Minutes Leo Délibes' celebrated "MARCHE DES CLOCHES" will be played.

Scene II.—THE WORKSHOP OF COPPÉLIUS.

AUTOMATON DANCE................ { **Mlle. LYDIA KYAKSHT**, Mme. ZANFRETTA, Mr. F. FARREN, and CORYPHÉES
VALSE COPPÉLIA, ADAGIO, BOLERO.............................. **Mlle. LYDIA KYAKSHT**
GRAND GALOP AND FINALE................. { **Mlle. LYDIA KYAKSHT**, Mme. ZANFRETTA, CORYPHÉES, and CORPS DE BALLET.

This scene begins with the entrance of the girls, led by Swanilda, who sets all the automatic figures to work, and generally make hay in the workshop. They are disturbed by the return of Coppelius and all fly, except Swanilda, who secretes herself behind an arras and takes the place of Coppelia the doll ; while the doll-maker is putting the place in order Franz, bent on solving the mystery of the doll, clambers through the window and is seized by Coppelius. At first inclined to punish him for his trespass, the old man decides to make use of him, gives him a sleeping potion, and, while insensible, endeavours to transfer the life from Franz to the supposed doll. Swanilda humours the old doll-maker, and he imagines that, following the instruction of a book of magic, he is making the doll do everything but talk. The arrival of Swanilda's friends and the Burgomaster cruelly dispel the illusion ; Franz awakens ; the lovers are reconciled ; and a purse of gold compensates Coppelius for the damage done to his figures.

FINALE MARCH ... "Sem|

Floral Decorations by ROBERT G

In accordance with the require- { The Public may leave at the end of the Performance by al
ments of the London County { The Fireproof Screen to the Proscenium Opening is lower
Council, { All Gangways, Passages, and Staircases must be kept free
Gentlemen are politely informed that Pip
The Management earnestly trust that Ladies will very kindly r

Musical Director—**Mr. CUTHBERT CLARKE.**

PRICES OF ADMISSION.—Private Boxes. 1 to 3 Guineas (all Box Tickets admit
Box Circle, 5s. (first three rows Numbered and Reserved).   Grand Circle (
No Re

Box Office (*Mr. J. E. Pickering*) open
Daily from 10 to 10.

Manager, Mr. H
Acting Manager,
Treasurer,

The authors of this book recall Madame Kyasht's company touring Britain before the 1939 war, helping to popularize classical dance, inspiring thousands of parents to enrol their children in local classes. The greatest apostle of ballet to ordinary audiences, in almost every corner of the globe, was the immortal Anna Pavlova. Whilst her legendary genius as a dancer is universally acknowledged, she is often accused of lack of taste or daring, of egocentric disregard for composers or innovators. It must, however, be recorded that among her designers were Joseph Urban, famous for his work for Ziegfeld and William Randolph Hearst, and Leon Bakst, who had created her costume for the famous *Dying Swan* as early as 1905. Whilst her repertoire was relatively unambitious, she is recorded as planning a 'ballet danced without music, but yet suggesting music in the imaginations of her

spectators' (according to the *New York Times*, 29 October 1915); and even more significantly, five years before Diaghilev mounted his famous London production of *The Sleeping Princess*, Pavlova presented a forty-five minute version of the famous ballet at the Hippodrome, New York, in 1916.

Bakst, who designed the production, held a special exhibition of his drawings at The Fine Art Society, the following year, when the catalogue explained – 'The Ballet of "La Belle aux Bois Dormant" has not been staged in this country. . . .' Pavlova, on that occasion, led the way for Diaghilev. She also revived *Giselle*, *Coppélia*, Petipa's *La Fille Mal Gardée*, as well as excerpts from *Raymonda*, *Don Quixote* and *La Bayadère*, keeping alive Russian classics which were only to regain full popular renewal with the Soviet companies, and through the enthusiasm of Rudolf Nureyev. Comparing Diaghilev's later search for novelties with Pavlova's conservatism (in both senses of the word), Arnold Haskell noted 'that it is his work and not hers that now appears old fashioned. . . . Her public was the whole world, his the coterie of pseudo aristocrats . . .' Nevertheless, Haskell conceded that whilst 'Pavlova has left a memory', Diaghilev left 'a school and a system'. It was on these premises of training and method, quite apart from his creative, aesthetic leads, that the whole of contemporary ballet has been founded.

In addition to Pavlova, another former member of the Ballets Russes established her own company during Diaghilev's life-time. Ida Rubinstein, the sensational success of *Cleopatra* and *Schéhérazade*, attracted wealthy lovers who financed her theatrical ambitions. These were initially a series of dramatic spectacles by the Italian poet d'Annunzio, and such eminent writers as Maeterlinck, Gide, Valery. Diaghilev regarded this initiative, and especially the contributions of Leon Bakst as her designer, as a form of dual

LEFT AND ABOVE

Pavlova and her company in *Assyrian Dance*, set to music by Saint-Saëns. *Photographs courtesy John Carr Doughty*

OPPOSITE

Bakst's costume for Ida Rubinstein in *Artemis Troublée*, 1922. *Collection Galleria del Levante, Milan*

disloyalty. When in 1928 she formed a ballet company, with Massine and Nijinska as her choreographers, and Alexandre Benois the chief designer, he feared lest these former colleagues, plus Rubinstein's seemingly unlimited resources, might not represent a serious rivalry. His fear was unfounded. The company continued until 1934, but Madame Rubinstein's beauty and elegance hardly compensated for her lack of talent as a dancer, whilst even her distinguished colleagues were unable to create any worthwhile additions to the balletic repertoire.

A far more serious threat to Diaghilev, and a more interesting indication of certain developments in the musical theatre, was the Ballets Suédois which functioned from 1920 to 1925. Formed by Rolf de Maré and Jean Börlin in Stockholm, its special character was firstly influenced by the

career of the Ballets Russes, but more specifically by the visit of Michel Fokine to Sweden, after his final break with Diaghilev. Fokine and his wife became close friends of Rolf de Maré, a wealthy and cultivated land-owner, whom they inspired to enact the role of a Swedish Maecenas; in turn Börlin became the Fokine of the new enterprise. There was, however, a major difference – the Swedes had no solid, classical, dance background; hence, as Bengt Häger, Director of Stockholm's Ballet Museum, wrote, 'The Ballets Suédois was, above all, the ballet of poets – Claudel, Cocteau, Cendras, Canudo'. This literary, satirical, worldly entertainment was enhanced by brilliant settings by Picabia and Leger, especially for *La Création du Monde* and *Relâche*.

In many respects, the element of satire or social comment in the entertainments of the Ballets Suèdois had much in common with German cabaret, and the brilliant Brecht-Weill operas. With little ballet tradition, as compared with opera, Germany was comparatively unaffected by the Ballets Russes. One can, however, discern some relationship between Diaghilev's style and that of Max Reinhardt, certainly in the splendour of presentation, but particularly in the famous mime-drama, *Sumurun*, with decors by Ernst Stern. This charming entertainment was clearly influenced by Diaghilev's oriental ballets, and in turn helped to popularize the theatrical form in musical revues in Paris and Broadway – and indeed Hollywood.

In later years German innovators, such as Kurt Jooss and Mary Wigmann, were to become seminal figures in the development of modern dance, certainly in America; Wigmann, in fact, arranged a version of *Sacré du Printemps* in a freer, Duncan-like manner, whilst more recently John Neumeier in Frankfurt mounted *The Firebird* as a science-fiction fantasy. The tradition and method of the Ballets Russes has reached Germany via England, since two of the Royal Ballet's most distinguished choreographers, Kenneth MacMillan and the late John Cranko virtually re-created the ballet companies of Berlin and Stuttgart on the lines of these two predecessors. MacMillan, in particular, restaged Russian classics notably a version of *The Sleeping Beauty*, with the designer Barry Kay, which re-established the specific Russian character of the work. This search for origins must also be noted in the efforts of that famous ex-patriot, Rudolf Nureyev to re-establish similar Russian classics, usually with splendid settings by Nicholas Georgiades.

So far as the original Ballets Russes is concerned, the death of Diaghilev resulted in a shocked hiatus. There was no question of 'The King is dead, long live the King'. Neither Lifar nor Kochno, the heirs apparent, were destined to reign alone – although Lifar immediately joined the Paris Opera, from where he undeniably affected the development of French ballet, and Kochno involved himself in some of the most interesting attempts to establish a company on Diaghilevian lines.

Especially important, both in France and throughout the world, was the dispersal of Russian dancers, choreographers, composers, designers, as

Act III from Kenneth MacMillan's 1967 version of *The Sleeping Beauty* for the Deutsche Oper, Berlin, with a 'Russian' setting by Barry Kay

apostles who formed touring companies, joined national ballets, and founded schools which trained future generations of dancers.

Eventually Diaghilev's mantle came to rest in Monte Carlo, for so many years his working headquarters. In 1931 René Blum, the Manager of the Monte Carlo theatre, and Colonel de Basil, a Cossack officer with a deep love of dance, formed the Ballets Russes de Monte Carlo. They reunited many of Diaghilev's former colleagues – Grigoriev, Kochno, Fokine, Massine, Balanchine, Nijinska, with Danilova, Markova and Vera Petrova as principal ballerinas. In time they produced a new generation of leading dancers, Toumanova, Riabouchinska, Baronova, Youskevich and Eglevsky, whilst in David Lichine – formerly with Pavlova and Rubinstein – they found a choreographer of note.

The company took over the former Ballets Russes repertoire, plus the existing scenery and costumes, thus keeping alive the ballets for younger audiences, and the artists who in their turn would re-stage or re-create these famous works. After three years the two partners split up – Blum, with Massine as artistic director, retained the company's name, operating largely in America. Colonel de Basil's group, led by Pavlova's husband Dandre, and Grigoriev, were first (confusingly) known as the Royal Covent Garden Ballet Russe, but eventually settled for the more accurate Ballets Russes de Colonel W. de Basil. Its claim to an historical niche lies in the fact that, stranded in Australia during the last war, it built on Pavlova's early tours (during which she engaged the young Robert Helpmann), to influence the establishment of the now flourishing Australian National Ballet.

In the meantime the exciting, but short lived, Ballets 33 had been created by the wealthy art collector Edward James for his Viennese wife Tilly Losch. Its brilliant collaborators included Balanchine, Milhaud, and the designers Derain, Berard and Tchelitchew. Kurt Weill created *The Seven Deadly Sins* which has since been adopted by many companies, including the Royal Ballet.

It should also be noted that as one result of the dispersal of Diaghilev's collaborators, and possibly in line with the broadened pattern of the Ballets Suèdois and the Ballets 33, the more sophisticated versions of popular revue now often included ballet sequences. It is interesting to note that ballet which entered England and other countries via the music-hall, was now returning through another branch of musical entertainment. C. B. Cochran, in particular, in the thirties, often included dance sequences by Balanchine, Massine, Lifar, with the help of brilliant designers like Berard.

Serge Lifar, who in the later years of the Ballets Russes had emerged as its newest star, re-established himself with the ballet *The Creatures of Prometheus*, to Beethoven's music, for the Paris Opera. He was to remain its *premier* dancer and *maître de ballet* from 1929 to 1959, exerting considerable influence on French ballet in general, and also occasionally establishing or working with independent companies. At the opera he produced over a

Baranova and Algeranoff in the de Basil production of *Le Coq d'Or*, 1937

Part of the programme of C. B. Cochran's revue *Still Dancing*, which included Massine's ballet *The Rake* with music by Roger Quilter, designs by William Nicholson; London Pavilion, 1925

EVENINGS at 8.30
MATINEES : TUESDAY and SATURDAY at 2.30

CHARLES B. COCHRAN'S
REVUE
"STILL DANCING"
By ARTHUR WIMPERIS and RONALD JEANS

Music by PHILIP BRAHAM, SISSLE & BLAKE, IVOR NOVELLO, MARC ANTHONY,
VIVIAN ELLIS, ISHAM JONES and IRVING BERLIN
Dialogue staged by ERNEST THESIGER
" THE RAKE," POMPEIAN BALLET and HUNGARIAN WEDDING
produced by LEONIDE MASSINE
All other Dances and Ensembles devised and produced by MAX RIVERS
The whole produced under the personal direction of **CHARLES B. COCHRAN**
*Mr. Charles B. Cochran begs to acknowledge his indebtedness to Mr. HERBERT MASON for his
invaluable help during the last stages of rehearsal*

PART I.

Scene 1. Lost Property Office.

Scene by JOHN BULL

Keeper of Lost Property Office	FRED WINN
A Reporter	LANCE LISTER
A Wife	JOAN CLARKSON
An Elderly Lady	VIOLET GOULD
A Chauffeur	NIGEL BRUCE
A Timid Gentleman	DOUGLAS BYNG
A Flash Young Lady	HERMIONE BADDELEY
A Stranger	ERNEST THESIGER

Miss Clarkson's Gown by TIZIANA, LTD.

Scene 2. Song " Poppy."　　　　　　　*Wimperis and Ellis*

ALICE DELYSIA
and
TERRI STORRI, GRETA BERONIUS, VERA BRYER, AVERIL HALEY, ROSE de
CORBETT NORANNA ROSE, NANCY BARNETT, NORA LORRIMORE, FLORENCE
DESMOND, BILLIE TEVLIN, LILIAN BOND, ANDREE CLAIRE, THALIA
BARBEROVA
WILLIAM CAVANAGH, BILLY REYNOLDS, KENNETH HENRY, FRED WALLACE,
RUPERT DOONE, DONALD NEVILLE
Mdlle Delysia's and Girls' Costumes by C. ALIAS, LTD.
Gentlemen's by MORRIS ANGEL & SON, LTD.
All designed by DORIS ZINKEISEN

Scene 3. " At the Fight."

Scene by MARC HENRI

Bill	DOUGLAS BYNG
Alf	NIGEL BRUCE
Sid	LANCE LISTER
Ivy	HERMIONE BADDELEY
Attendant	ERNEST THESIGER
A Lady	JOAN CLARKSON
Her Son	HERBERT RICHARDS
M.C.	ERNEST LINDSAY

Scene 4. " Still Dancing."

The Hussars	ROSE de CORBETT NANCY BARNETT LILIAN BOND THALIA BARBEROVA
Danse Eccentrique	FLORENCE DESMOND
Valse Moderne	GRETA BERONIUS
The Faun	TERRI STORRI
Old Moscow	VERA BRYER

The
Rivers Rag { BILLIE TEVLIN, FLORENCE DESMOND, ANDREE CLAIRE,
NORANNA ROSE, TERRI STORRI, ROSE DE CORBETT, LILIAN
BOND, GRETA BERONIUS, AVERIL HALEY, THALIA BARBEROVA,
VERA BRYER, NANCY BARNETT
Costumes designed by DORIS ZINKEISEN, executed by L. & H. NATHAN

Scene 5. " Number 13 "　　Scene by JOHN BULL

Ruby	HERMIONE BADDELEY
Young Doctor	NIGEL BRUCE
A Postman	ERNEST LINDSAY
A Lady Journalist	JOAN CLARKSON

Miss Clarkson's Gown by TIZIANA, LTD.

Scene 6. " The Rake."　　　　　　*A Hogarth Impression*

Choreography by LEONIDE MASSINE.　Music by ROGER QUILTER.
Costumes designed and scene painted by WILLIAM NICHOLSON
Scene built by JOHN BULL and Costumes made by ALIAS.　Masks by BETTY MUNTZ.
Massine has taken a number of Hogarth's characters—symbolic and realistic.
William Nicholson has given them a characteristic environment for a Hogarthian Orgy.
" The Rake " lolls drunkenly in a chair while his wanton companions disport around him.　The
negro Cupid is busy with bow and arrows, plumbing the hearts of his victims' and the worship
of women and wine whips itself up into a passionate whirl.　And while the revellers seek their
pleasure, the sages are wrapt in contemplation of their globe, and a window frames the faces
of a curious crowd, who see, and are silent.

OPERA GLASSES MAY BE HIRED FROM THE THEATRE ATTENDANTS 6d. EACH

hundred original works, but more importantly he raised the company to new standards of excellence. In a brief break with the Opera he established Les Nouveaux Ballets de Monte Carlo in 1945, in which Diaghilev's shadow can be discerned in Lifar's use of music by Strauss, Tcherepnine, Mussorgsky and Prokofiev. Two years later the company was taken over by the Marquis de Cuevas, who with some style and flourish re-established a (short-lived) touring ballet on the lines of the original Ballets Russes.

In 1946 Boris Kochno, Diaghilev's former secretary, founded Les Ballets des Champs Elysées, in which Massine and Lichine played leading roles, as well as the emergent French choreographer, Roland Petit. This group had a brilliant career, with a number of outstanding young dancers, Renée Jeanmaire, Janine Charrat, Jean Babilée (all of whom studied with Russian teachers), and a series of popular successes which included *Carmen*, *Les Forains*, the silent *La Création*, and the sensational Cocteau ballet *Le Jeune Homme et la Mort*. Berard and Clavé contributed superb settings.

Modern French ballet, as personified by the work of Roland Petit and Maurice Bejart, exemplifies the spectacular side of Diaghilev's work, the uninhibited desire to please, entertain and excite in purely theatrical terms, without over-anxiety for philosophical or social messages.

It is, however, in Britain that one traces a direct line of cause and effect, from the first appearances of the Russians, between 1908 and 1911, to the eventual creation of the Royal Ballet – as well as the flourishing Ballet Rambert and London Festival Ballet. Both Pavlova and Diaghilev favoured the employment of British dancers, whom they found more disciplined, more compliant, ready to learn and to act as part of a team. As early as 1911 the London *Times* hoped native dancers might 'arrive at some imitation of it [the Ballets Russes] on our own stage'; and Diaghilev himself forecast, 'These English are fine dancers, one day they will form a school of their own'. Ninette de Valois, Alicia Markova, Anton Dolin, and also Robert Helpmann, received important experience from the Russians, not only as performers but also as pupils. Markova and Dolin, and later Margot Fonteyn, were students with Astafieva, the first Russian to open a school in London.

The deaths of Diaghilev and Pavlova, in 1929 and 1931 respectively, released, so to speak, a number of gifted English dancers. In 1930 two prototype groups emerged – the Ballet Club, begun by Marie Rambert (who worked with Nijinsky on *Le Sacre du Printemps*), who in 1920 founded her London school, and the Camargo Society, created by the ballet critic Arnold Haskell and P. J. S. Richardson, editor of *The Dancing Times*. Rambert, in particular, must be credited with training the first generation of English dancers – Pearl Argyll, Andrée Howard, Prudence Hyman, Maude Lloyd, Harold Turner and William Chappell; and in Frederick Ashton, the first important British choreographer, later to succeed Dame Ninette de Valois as Director of the Royal Ballet.

The two groups joined forces in a series of historic ballet programmes.

By this time Ninette de Valois was also active. At the age of 25, already established on the London stage, she joined the Ballets Russes from 1923 to 1925. Her purpose, she later explained, was 'to study production . . . to acquire a working knowledge of existing ballets, and last, but not least, to escape . . . from the commercial theatre'. Of Diaghilev, she commented, 'He made me aware of a new world, a world that held the secrets of that aesthetic knowledge I'd been looking for'. Back in England she founded her own school and produced ballets for the Abbey Theatre, Dublin and the Festival Theatre, Cambridge. With the Camargo Society and her own troupe, she founded, in 1931, the Vic-Wells Company, from which emerged the Sadlers Wells Ballet and later, in 1956, the now famous Royal Ballet at Covent Garden. Markova and Dolin, also Diaghilev-trained, were her first stars, plus Pearl Argyll and Frederick Ashton, and then the great partnership of Fonteyn and Helpmann. Constant Lambert, from whom Diaghilev had commissioned the score for *Romeo and Juliet*, was her musical director.

Thus, it can be claimed that the roots of the Royal Ballet go deep into the Russian achievement – Diaghilev was the original inspiration of Ninette de Valois, and his company set standards of training and performance, as well as an artistic and theatrical ethos, which have always influenced the British company. Whilst the Royal Ballet has produced a number of brilliant choreographers – de Valois, Ashton, and the present director Kenneth Macmillan – it has never neglected Russian sources. Dame Ninette herself recreated *Barabau* and *The Gods Go A'Begging*, and many other Russian works have been restaged – the ever-popular *Les Sylphides, La Péri, Le Sacre du Printemps, L'Après-midi d'un Faune, The Good Humoured Ladies,*

Firebird, The Prodigal Son – sometimes calling on the collaboration of their originators, such as Benois, Massine, Balanchine, as well as inspiring new interpretations. Above all the Royal Ballet called on Nijinska to stage her masterpieces, Les Noces and Les Biches, with the original settings by Gontcharova and Marie Laurencin. The ghost of Diaghilev must feel a great debt to Dame Ninette and her successors.

In its early years the Ballet Rambert preserved many Russian works in its repertoire, but more recently it has devoted itself to experimental dance. The newly formed Scottish National Ballet has also re-staged Diaghilev originals, combining classical and modern forms. It is, however, the London Festival Ballet which shows a special devotion to the memory of the Ballets Russes. Founded in 1949 to back Markova and Dolin, the company inherited from those two dancers the brave, barn-storming spirit of Pavlova in taking the classical repertoire to a broader public. They have re-staged many favourites of the Ballets Russes – La Péri, Le Spectre, Les Sylphides, enlisting the services of Grigoriev and Massine, and the Russian ballerinas Riabouchinska and Danilova, both as performers and teachers. Even more interesting have been the revivals of Prince Igor, Schéhérazade, Petrushka and Le Tricorne, using the original artists' designs.

The American scene, often more varied and more daring than British ballet, has also been deeply affected by Diaghilev. The Ballets Russes made two important American tours, which among other things encouraged Russian dancers to settle in the country. Adolph Bolm formed his Intimate Ballet, and as early as 1918 and 1919 staged versions of Le Coq d'Or and Petrushka in Chicago. Another dancer, Gavrilov, became Director of Ballet Theatre, and Theodore Kosloff, who had appeared with Karsavina in London in 1909, became famous as a silent film star in Hollywood, where he opened a ballet school for which a fellow Russian, Erté, designed a delightful poster.

Michael Mordkin, Pavlova's partner, founded a company in New York, whilst Boris Romanov, choreographer of La Tragédie de Salomé, brought his

ABOVE LEFT

Nijinska's famous ballet Les Noces restaged for the Royal Ballet, with the original designs by Gontcharova

ABOVE RIGHT

Rudolf Nureyev as The Prodigal Son with Deanne Bergsma in the Royal Ballet production

OPPOSITE TOP

Chagall's backcloth for The Firebird, New York City Ballet, 1949

OPPOSITE BELOW

Christian Berard's setting for The Seventh Symphony, Scene III, choreography by Massine, Les Ballets de Monte Carlo, Théâtre du Monte Carlo, 1938

Fashion drawing by Romme, from *Les Feuillets d'Art*, 1919

Galina Samtsova and Dudley von Loggenburg in the London Festival Ballet's production of *Petrushka*, based on Benois' designs researched by Geoffrey Guy

The London Festival Ballet's version of *Schéhérazade*, based on Bakst's original costumes researched by Geoffrey Guy. Jean Pierre Alban as the Shah

The Polovtsian Dances from *Prince Igor*, recreated by the London Festival Ballet from Roerich's original designs; with Freya Dominic and Dudley von Loggenburg

BELOW

The Three Cornered Hat, with Picasso's original designs, in the London Festival Ballet production

Ballet Romantique to the Metropolitan. Other Russians, Wilzak, Schollar, even the great Nijinska, opened ballet schools in America. Fokine ended his career in the United States, dying there in 1942; like Massine he contributed much to the musical stage, apart from his association with de Basil.

It was the arrival of the Ballets Russes de Monte Carlo in 1933 which set in motion later developments. As Arnold Haskell wrote, 'the conspicuous success for five years of de Basil forced the Metropolitan to open its doors to the American Ballet'.

After the outbreak of the 1939 war a number of Russian dancers settled in the United States, with the result, according to Lifar, that 'the American ballet became virtually semi-Russian'; from 1929, in fact, Fokine, Massine, Nijinska and Lichine had produced an enormous repertoire for American companies and audiences, often revivals of Diaghilev ballets. A more indigenous 'Yankee' style also emerged – not only based on Isadora Duncan and Ruth St Denis, through Martha Graham and her successors, but a fusion of Russian techniques with more experimental choreography, and the uninhibited borrowings from other art media. The relaxed, often daring American work of Jerome Robbins, Glen Tetley, Alvin Ailey, and other gifted choreographers, is, in part, a mixture of Russian and native forces.

The prime source of the Diaghilev strain in American ballet is, of course, Georges Balanchine. Although trained in the Imperial Russian school as a choreographer, he established his individuality with Diaghilev, for whom he produced ten ballets. These are especially noteworthy for their collaboration with Stravinsky, the composer Balanchine has often turned to in his American career. After spells with the Danish Royal Ballet and the short-

LEFT

Salvador Dali's curtain for *Bacchanale*, Massine's ballet for Les Ballets de Monte Carlo, Metropolitan Opera House, New York, 1939

Dali's curtain for *Labyrinth*, Massine's
ballet for Les Ballets de Monte Carlo,
Metropolitan Opera House, New York,
1941

lived Ballets 33, Balanchine went to the United States at the invitation of
Lincoln Kirstein to found a school and a permanent group. Within two
years he was at the Metropolitan Opera, and after working on Broadway
and Hollywood films he established the world famous New York City
Ballet in 1948. Of his Diaghilev period, *Apollo* and *The Prodigal Son* have
retained their popularity, whilst in his later career Balanchine produced a
number of new masterpieces, including *Ballet Imperial* and *Agon*. Typical of
his Ballets Russes revivals is a new version of *The Firebird* with decor by
another Russian, Marc Chagall, himself once a pupil of Bakst.

It is unnecessary to sum up Diaghilev's role in making ballet into an
international art form. He provided the main impetus for national and
private companies in all parts of the world – not only in Europe and the
United States, but in South America which his company visited, and even
Japan which only knew of Diaghilev by proxy.

LA BELLE SANS NOM, Nouvelle, par Jean Rameau

7 DIAGHILEV'S INFLUENCE ON FASHION & DECORATION

by Martin Battersby

'There are many indications in periodicals specializing in the fine and decorative arts that the Russian Ballet had a wide effect, a remarkable influence on fashion and the decorative arts. One production in particular – *Schéhérazade* – created the most profound impression. No other ballet before or since has succeeded in impressing itself on the imaginations of its audiences to such a degree. Jacques-Emile Blanche in *Les Arts Plastiques* wrote that 'the first performance was an important evening for the theatre, for dressmakers, for interior decorators, for jewellers and for all branches of decoration. It is difficult to realize today the metamorphosis which transformed the decorative arts.' Blanche was writing – in 1931 – of the effect upon Parisian audiences; in London where interest in the decorative arts was not considered so necessary as in Paris, a contributor to *The Studio* recorded that in 1914 'for a time Art has danced to the strains of the Russian Ballet leaving here and there lingering notes on dress fabrics, wallpapers and cushions'.

Paris and Islam were not strangers before the dazzling premiere of *Schéhérazade* on 10 June 1910. The unquenchable thirst of the French aristocracy for exotic novelties had aroused interest in the Near East, as well as in the artifacts of the remoter civilizations of China and Japan. During the seventeenth and eighteenth centuries decorative elements from these countries had been incorporated into the baroque and rococo styles. Napoleon's conquests in the Near East brought about a new enthusiasm for Turkish as well as Egyptian art – and in the following decades the Islamic countries of North Africa, easily accessible to France, attracted a throng of writers and artists – Delacroix, Vernet, Chateaubriand, Hugo, Gautier, Chassériau, Flaubert, Dehodencq, Constant, Clarin . . . all had travelled extensively in the Near East, recording in words and paint their impressions of its picturesque life. But Islam was largely eclipsed during the latter part of the nineteenth century by the newly available wealth of inspiration to be found in Japanese art after the opening of that country to the West. Art Nouveau, derived largely from Japanese influences, diminished still further the interest in the Near East although this new style and the Arabian Nights came together briefly in Orazi's decorations for a story 'La Belle sans Nom' published in the 1900 Christmas number of *Figaro*.

The oriental ballets of Diaghilev were not the only spectacles in this genre to be seen in Paris at the time. *Kismet*, by Edward Knoblock, originally written as a vehicle for Sir Henry Irving in 1909 – a year before *Schéhérazade* – was given in a final version in 1911 in London and New York; and a French translation starring Lucien Guitry had its premiere in Paris in 1912. Max Reinhardt's *Sumurun* was another sumptuous oriental fantasy pre-

La Belle sans Nom, illustration by Orazi in the Christmas number of *Le Figaro Illustré*, 1900

sented in Paris at the same time as *Schéhérazade*. Neither of these caught the imagination of the theatre-going public to the same degree as the Russian Ballet, and credit must go to the decorative genius of Léon Bakst.

The most immediate influence was upon fashion and here the brilliant, egocentric couturier, Paul Poiret, added his contribution in creating what

George Sheringham described as 'those delightful svelte creatures who seemed suddenly to come into existence . . . the product of all things Persian . . . Persian costume . . . Persian patterns, hairdressings and head-dress'. In his fascinating but unreliable memoirs Poiret waxes indignant over the credit given to Bakst for the oriental fashions of 1910/1911. A legendary Baghdad was much in tune with Poiret's taste for the luxurious and bizarre – a taste which was in the end to lead to his ruin; but equally that mysterious coincidence – so characteristic of the fashion world – played a part.

Poiret could assert with truth that as a couturier with a growing reputation, and a not inconsiderable flair for publicity, he was in a stronger position to influence fashion than Bakst, but few elegant Parisians cared who was the originator of their new draped dresses, the rich and elaborate fabrics, the dashing 'jupes-culottes'. Jupes-culottes were forecast as fashions of the future by Paul Poiret in his beautifully produced booklet 'Les Choses de Paul Poiret' issued for publicity in 1911; four drawings by Georges Lepape showed models for tennis, gardening, day and evening wear which combined the current high-waisted silhouette with trousers

Autumn Fashions 1914, advertisement illustration

OPPOSITE TOP LEFT

Georges Lepape's drawing of a model by Paul Poiret, from *Gazette du Bon Ton* 1913

OPPOSITE RIGHT

Eightpence a Mile, revue at the Alhambra Theatre, London, designed by Paul Poiret, *c.* 1913

OPPOSITE BELOW

La Jupe Culotte, from a postcard with postmark of 1911. *Collection Martin Battersby*

gathered into bands round the ankles – a bolder fashion than all but a few chic Parisiennes were prepared to adopt. Usually the models to be seen at fashionable Longchamps and other elegant race-meetings were more discreet, the trouser effect being partly concealed by draped folds of fabric so that in repose the line was that of a harem skirt. Less daring was a tunic or over-dress with a wired hem which gave a satisfactorily oriental effect when the wearer was standing up, but which must have been awkward when sitting.

The usual accompaniment to both these creations was a draped turban of fabric with an upstanding tuft of aigrettes. A 'Durbar-Turban' decorated with aigrettes priced at 30,000 francs was illustrated in *Fémina* in 1912, with the suggestion that a less costly imitation could be made at home by using

stiffened chiffon. The fashion writer Jeanne Tournier advised her readers seeking inspiration for evening turbans to visit another Oriental-inspired play *Les Trois Sultanes*. It is possible that Jeanne Lanvin, in her alternative career as an interior decorator, found inspiration for Persian head-dresses when designing the lighting fixtures for the Théâtre Danou (reminiscent of the encrusted ornament on a Bakst costume) which accompanied the designer's gilded sculptured ornament on a blue background.

151

The Delhi Durbar of 1911 was widely featured in the French periodicals and served as proof that the theatrical splendours of the Russian Ballet had their counterpart in real life. The fabulous richness of the coronation of George V and Queen Mary as Emperor and Empress of India, the homage of bejewelled princes and maharajahs (many of whose splendid jewels had been reset in Paris for the occasion) excited the imaginations of Parisian hostesses. A correspondent recorded in *Fémina* during 1912 that,

the influence of the Orient has been exercised so strongly on our tastes and fashions that inevitably the idea should occur to give costume balls on the themes of the Thousand and One Nights. The famous Jupes-Culottes, the celebrations of the crowning of George V in India, the sumptuous ballets at the Châtelet with their presentation of the Asiatic legends of *Thamar, Schéhérazade, Le Dieu Bleu* and *L'Oiseau de Feu* in a magnificent richness of costume have aroused a desire – even a need – for masquerades in a similar style reproducing the same prodigality of mis-en-scene.

No expense was spared in decor or costumes for these entertainments. Poiret's 'Thousand and Second Night's Ball' has often been described, and this was followed by at least two which received much attention in the press for the extravagance of their presentation. Aristocratic Parisiennes of un-impeachable respectability vied with each other as langourous odalisques or sultry inmates of a seraglio. Inevitably the majority were almost direct copies of designs by Bakst – the *bayadères* in *Le Dieu Bleu* inspired several ladies to appear as temple prostitutes with stuffed peacocks perched precariously on their shoulders.

Turbanned and harem-skirted Parisiennes found at their disposal a new selection of exotic perfumes. Delicate flower scents, hitherto regarded as

permissible for a respectable woman – only *cocottes* could advertise their presence by a cloud of sandalwood, patchouli or other sultry odours – were superseded by headier perfumes; as a contemporary advertisement enthused, 'by wearing "Sakountala" or "Nirvana" she could envelope herself in a voluptuous aroma recalling the atmosphere of the Russian Ballets, evoking memories of the seductive dancing and decorations of *Schéhérazade*'. Paul Poiret, possibly the first couturier to make a profitable side-line from scents, which he collectively called *Les Parfums Rosine*, turned to the Orient for their individual names: 'Maharajah', 'Nuit de Chine', 'L'Estrange Fleur', 'La Coupe d'Or' and 'Le Fruit Défendu' carried suggestions of exotic perversities. Lubin's *Kismet* obviously cashed in on the success of the play of the same name.

The trend toward colourful jewellery to which Jacques-Emile Blanche referred occurred after the war. Designers had introduced coloured stones combined with enamels around 1900, and most notably René Lalique had broken new ground in setting off the hue and brilliance of specimen stones with motifs of carved glass and delicately wrought metalwork in his master-pieces. The passing of Art Nouveau had resulted in a return to common-

153

place diamond-set jewellery timidly based on eighteenth-century designs, and Lalique abandoned his coloured jewels to concentrate on glass working. The short period after the premieres of the Russian Ballets gave comparatively little opportunity for jewellers to follow the quasi-oriental trends, but after the war the influx into Paris of foreign visitors and an advantageous rate of exchange gave an impetus to the creation of rich and exotic baubles. Carved Indian emeralds, rubies and sapphires were combined with diamonds in massive brooches, bracelets and earrings which could have decked Zobeide, the heroine of *Schéhérazade*, or the cruel Thamar. Long ropes of pearls ending in tassels of seed pearls, were set off by deep red Persian corals or black onyx. For the less affluent, imitation pearls, such as those sold under the name Indra, served as a substitute. Tassels were used as never before; not only were they applied in silk and golden profusion to dresses and evening cloaks – often in the most unlikely places – but silver bullion was also used to give a harem touch to lampshades and cushions, and in some cases replaced metal handles on furniture.

The oriental influence on the actual shape of clothes was transitory, for the essence of fashion is change and the assimilation of new ideas. The leaders of fashion soon abandoned the turbans, harem skirts and kimono wraps when these were taken up by a wider public; and in any case the advent of war brought about general simplification. The novelty of appearing as a chic odalisque soon wore off, but the richly patterned fabrics and the brilliant colours continued to hold sway.

Rich colours were the most lasting legacy of the Russian Ballet in both fashion and interior decoration. 'It may be said that the Russian Ballet has introduced to the English stage delirious colour that has never been surpassed' wrote Huntly Carter in an issue of the appropriately named periodical *Colour* for October 1915; and his comment could equally well have applied to the English home. Since the late nineties and the heyday of Art Nouveau the predominating harmonies in dress and interior decoration had been the muted opalescent tones of moonstones, mother of pearl, ivory and sycamore. Pale rose, green, mauve or blue were shadowed as though seen through a layer of grey chiffon, and strong colours were subdued and low in tone. Even when Art Nouveau had largely fallen out of favour in the early years of the century this tendency lingered.

Bakst, with his designs for *Thamar, Les Orientales, Le Dieu Bleu* and of course *Schéhérazade*, assaulted Parisian eyes with a dazzling richness of pure colour and unconventional harmonies derived from Persian and Indian sources. Overnight the intense blue of turquoises, lapis-lazuli and sapphires, the reds of vermilion lacquer, rubies and coral, the shades of orange to be found in fire-opals, zinnias and marigolds, greens taken from emeralds, malachite or verdigris, sharp intense yellows, purples and violets evoked from amythysts, grapes and aubergines were used singly or combined in dazzling juxtaposition with liberal additions of gold or silver. Such colours and combinations of colours had not been seen for fifty years or more, since

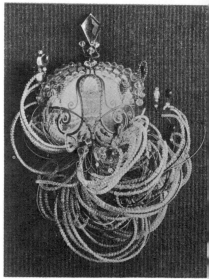

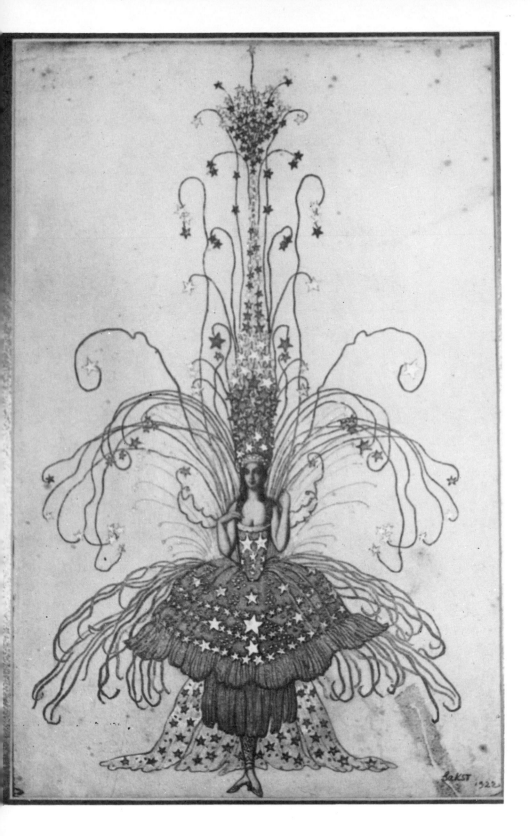

the days of the Second Empire when the invention of aniline dyes had opened up a new range of brilliant and even harsh colours which were much to the taste of the *nouveau riche* society of the day. Although in flowers and the plumage of birds the most unexpected colour harmonies can be found, for some mysterious reason fashion had considered in doubtful taste such combinations of colours as blue and green or cerise with orange. Two shades of the same colour – for instance crimson and vermilion – were not considered possible together. Bakst and the other Russian designers ignored such niceties and their daring use of such combinations opened the eyes of the West to new beauties.

It was not that Bakst and his companions invented new colours. To those familiar with the Orient, and even certain periods of European art, these unconventional juxtapositions of brilliant colour were obviously derived from Persia, India and Turkey. Furthermore in Paris the *Fauves* – Matisse, van Dongen, Rouault and Dufy – had used equally strong colours since 1906, but despite critical acclaim their impact was limited to a small group of admirers and patrons. The canvases of the *Fauves* remained compositions enclosed in a frame. The designs of the Russian Ballet, presented at fashionable and highly publicized theatrical occasions, serving as background for brilliant dancing and exciting music, had a far greater impact on its audience. Bakst's 'debauch of colour' as a French critic described it, with an added accent on female nudity, which if it did not actually appear on the stage was stressed in the widely reproduced costume designs, spread far beyond the limits of the theatre to become part of everyday life for the next twenty years or more.

Some indication of the tendency toward a more adventurous use of colour in fashion can be found by examining captions in the popular French periodical *Fémina*. It contained a considerable number of pages on the latest fashions, both in photographs and in drawings; in common with the majority of its contemporaries very few indications were given as to the identity of the designers of the clothes. Colour was only used on rare occasions so that the readers were dependent on the captions for full details. In the months immediately preceding the first 1909 season of the Russian Ballet in Paris the dresses are described as being in muted and even sombre colours – navy blue, myrtle green, grey, olive green, prune and 'khaki'. In a large number of cases there is no indication of either colour or fabric. By 1911 this had completely changed. Almost without exception the colours are meticulously described, shades distinguished by names such as 'Rose Vif', 'Nuits d'Orient', 'Begonia Rose', 'Cerise', 'Tabac' and 'Blond', in addition to the self-explanatory tints like 'Jonquil' or 'Delft Blue'. The muted shades of a year or so before have been replaced by a gamut of brilliant colours. This trend is confirmed in the colour plates of the luxury fashion magazine *Le Gazette du Bon Ton*, which first appeared in 1912.

In the same year two other fashion magazines appeared, *Le Journal des*

Dames et des Modes and *Modes et Manières*. A number of young and talented illustrators were encouraged to record fashion in their own individual styles. These brilliant draughtsmen were young enough to be captivated by the decorative aspects of the Russian Ballet while the new fashion magazines gave them unlimited scope for recording the latest whims of fashion, from frivolous fantasies of ribbons and artificial flowers, to the more serious business of impressing a new line upon the public. The manufacturers of the new scents and cosmetics enlisted their services for advertisements, while several of them imaginatively illustrated volumes containing poems in praise of Karsavina or Nijinsky by Jean Cocteau and others. A young would-be poet and artist named Charles de Bestigui, later to become one of the most notable art patrons of the century, produced a privately published book of verses, *Songeries*, his own illustrations embellished with gold reflecting an enthusiasm for the oriental ballets of Diaghilev.

The arrival of the Russian Ballet in Paris coincided with the emergence of a host of young, talented and extremely versatile decorative designers. Mention has been made of fashion illustrators, but it must be stressed that they worked in many other fields. In England versatility was, and still is, regarded with suspicion, but in Paris the opposite has always been the case. Fashion and interior decoration were closely linked with the theatre, and it was inevitable that the oriental trend should pervade the decorative arts. Fortunately a number of cultured and discriminating rich patrons existed who chose all the accessories of living with the same care that they had devoted to their clothes. Designers of textiles, furniture, ironwork, glass and book-bindings were among the enthusiastic audiences who succumbed to the magic of Diaghilev. Even the war years were only a temporary lull in the outburst of creative activity which characterized the period 1910 to 1914; after the Armistice it continued with undiminished brilliance, encouraged by the economic need to reassert Paris as pre-eminent in all branches of the arts. That the inspiration of Diaghilev and Bakst was a major influence in this flowering was acknowledged by the critic and art historian Gabriel Moury as late as 1925: 'There is no doubt that the influence of the Russian Ballet not only in theatrical design but on fashion, book production, textile design and indeed upon all the arts is as strong today as it was in 1910.'

Where decoration was concerned the strongest reflection of the trend could be seen in the products of Paul Poiret's Atelier Martine. Most of the Martine wallpapers, textiles, carpets and decorative schemes betray the oriental leanings of Poiret himself. Other designers – Ruhlmann, Groult, Follot, Dufrêne, to mention only the most notable contemporaries – also reveal the influence of the Russian Ballet. The use of rich and vibrating colour derived from Bakst's designs was a common factor, as was a penchant for rare woods and unusual materials such as vellum and shagreen, while the bold patterns of the textiles lavishly embellished with gold and silver lent an element of sensuousness.

In England no such striking transformation had taken place in the

Two illustrations by Charles de Bestigui for his privately printed book of poems, 1914

decorative arts. More conservative than French taste and far less eager for change, English taste still remained faithful to the Tudor, Queen Anne and Chippendale styles. Appreciation of the exotic and barbaric aspects of Diaghilev's ballets was no less in London than in Paris, but there was little or no inclination to incorporate them into daily life. The visits of the Russians did comparatively little to shake English preference for the products of a remoter Orient; Chinese and Japanese artifacts remained unchallenged accompaniments to oak, walnut and mahogany. But in one respect at least Bakst had an effect upon the English home and that was in the use of brighter colours. A Heal's advertisement of 1919 declared: 'The drab English home is fast being relegated to the limbo of a more prosaic age. Perhaps the most notable advance in home decoration is shown in the

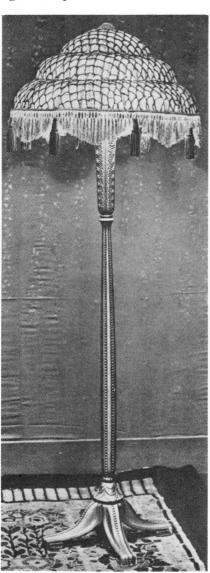

courage displayed in the selection of bright and joyous fabrics and schemes of gay colour decoration.' A 'joyous' fabric in either 'Bagdad' or 'Tabdar' ranges – both described as being 'in the brilliant colours of the Orient' – could be purchased at Liberty's at 5/11 a yard. In 1916 a room was described as follows: 'A floor stained purple, lemon yellow walls, half concealed by orange satin draperies, furniture smothered under a plethora of sky-blue, sea-green and daffodil cushions lavishly embroidered with crowns in gold thread and a pale lemon grand piano on a dais hung with yellow satin and canopied with axure shot with silver', with the added comment that this room was unusual even for unconventional Chelsea.

Colour and Interior Decoration, written by the architect Basil Ionides, with colour plates after paintings by William Ranken, demonstrates a typical compromise in which a flood of intense colour was allowed to invade the walls of a room whose furniture and accessories remain as traditional as ever. Another example of this is *The Orange Room*, a painting by Davis Richter – the vivid colour of the walls would have been inadmissible before the advent of *Schéhérazade*. The Ionides book devotes considerable space to the treatment, from a practical as well as psychological angle, of red, blue, orange, green, silver, gold as a foil to black and all-white rooms (considerably antedating Syrie Maugham's more publicized creations). Large areas of bright colour were featured in designs by Shirley Wainwright in *The Studio* in 1921, for the appropriately named Oriental Cafe and the Sesame Cafe. (Teashops with pseudo-oriental atmospheres were opened by distressed gentlewomen in the twenties as an alternative to the genteel Tudor Tearooms.)

A noticeable feature of advertisements during the twenties was the prominence given to cushions – not the huge affairs of gold lamé and

brocade so lavishly used in French interiors – but smaller, more sedate shapes covered in combinations of Roman stripes and plain fabrics, tastefully trimmed with discreet gold braidings, and invariably described as 'gay' cushions. In more Bohemian households these were often used as substitutes for conventional seating; a Punch cartoon of the period shows a couple, the wife Eton-cropped in a fashionably skimpy evening dress, the husband, thick-necked, balding, uncomfortable in his dinner jacket, both sitting on cushions on the floor drinking Turkish coffee. The long-suffering husband asks plaintively, 'I say, Monica, let's leave Chelsea and sit on chairs again'.

By the mid-twenties the craze for oriental decoration had waned, partly through over familiarity and because newer themes were in the air. The Russian Ballet still held their sway over audiences but the later works had little or no influence on the decorative arts. The comparative failure of *Le Dieu Bleu* convinced Diaghilev that the vein of Indo-Persian inspiration had been worked out and that a public avid for novelty, and particularly a French public, could only be satisfied by a continual stream of new and original offerings. Instead of dictating fashion Diaghilev was following it. Bakst, Benois and other designers of the early ballets had the impact of novelty and unfamiliarity, while subsequent designers, however talented, were already known to part of the audiences. Important ballets were created, some still in the repertoire, but none succeeded in influencing fashion and decoration as *Schéhérazade* had done.

CHRONOLOGY

BIBLIOGRAPHY

INDEX

CHRONOLOGY

1872	Born Novgorod
1874	Moved to St Petersburg
1882	Moved to Perm, where he was brought up on his grandfather's estate
1890	St Petersburg – joined Alexandre Benois and his friends
1893	First European tour
1897	First European exhibition, Stieglitz Museum, St Petersburg
1898	Russo-Finnish exhibition
1899	Founded *World of Art*
	Appointed assistant to Director, Imperial Theatres and edited Year Book
	International Exhibition, Academy of Fine Arts
1904	*World of Art* ceased publication
1905	Portraits Exhibition, Tauride Palace
1906	Russian Exhibition, Salon d'Automne, Grand Palais, Paris
1907	Russian concerts, Paris
1908	*Boris Godunov*, Paris Opera
1909	Season of Opera and Ballet. Théâtre du Châtelet, Paris: *Les Sylphides, Cléopâtre, Le Festin, Le Pavillon d'Armide, Prince Igor, Ivan the Terrible, Russlan and Ludmilla*
1910	Season Paris Opera. First collaboration with Stravinsky. *Schéhérazade, l'Oiseau de Feu, Carnaval, Giselle, Les Orientales*
1911	Seasons in Rome, Monte Carlo, Paris, Covent Garden London
	Founding of Diaghilev's own company
	Petrushka, Le Spectre de la Rose, Narcisse, Sadko, Swan Lake, Aurora and the Prince (from *The Sleeping Princess*).
1912	*Daphnis et Chloé, Thamar, Le Dieu Bleu, l'Après-midi d'un Faune*
1913	Seasons in Monte Carlo, Paris, London, first South American tour
	Nijinsky's marriage
	Fokine's resignation
	Le Sacre du Printemps, Jeux, La Tragédie de Salomé, Boris Godunov, La Nuit de Mai
1914	Fokine returns. Seasons in Paris and London
	Le Coq d'Or, La Légende de Joseph, Papillons, Midas, Le Rossignol
1915	Diaghilev in Italy and Switzerland. Charity gala, Paris.
	First tour of United States
1916	*Le Soleil de Nuit*

Seasons in Italy, Switzerland, Spain

Triana, España, Histoires Naturelles, Kikimora, Las Meninas, Till Eulenspiegel, Sadko (new version)

1917   Seasons in Italy, Spain, Portugal, South America

First collaboration with Picasso

Les Femmes de Bonne Humeur, Contes Russes, Parade, Feu d'Artifice (Fireworks)

1918   London season

Cléopâtre (new Delaunay setting), *Les Jardins d'Aranjuez*

1919   Seasons London, Manchester, Paris

La Boutique Fantasque, The Three-Cornered Hat, l'Oiseau et le Prince (from *Sleeping Beauty*)

1920   Seasons in London, Paris

Le Chant du Rossignol, Pulcinella, Le Astuzie Femminili, Le Sacre du Printemps (new choreography Massine)

1921   Seasons in London, Paris

The Sleeping Princess, Cuadro Flamenco, Chout

1922   Season Paris, tours of France and Belgium

Le Mariage d'Aurore (Sleeping Beauty), *Le Renard, Mavra*

1923   Season Paris. Settles in Monte Carlo and forms Les Ballets Russes de Monte Carlo

Les Noces

1924   Seasons Paris, London, Monte Carlo

Les Biches, Les Fâcheux, Mercure, Les Tentations de la Bergère, Cimarosiana, Le Train Bleu, Night on the Bare Mountain, Le Médecin Malgré Lui, Philémon et Baucis

1925   Seasons London, Paris

Les Matelots, Zéphyr et Flore, Barabau, Le Chant du Rossignol (choreography Balanchine)

1926   Seasons London, Paris, Berlin, Turin, Milan, Monte Carlo

Jack-in-the-Box, La Pastorale, Romeo and Juliet, The Triumph of Neptune, La Colombe, l'Education Manqué

1927   London, Paris, tours of Germany, Austria, Hungary, Czechoslovakia, Switzerland

Le Pas d'Acier, La Chatte, Mercure, Œdipus Rex

1928   London, Paris, Belgium

Ode, Apollon Musagètes, The Gods Go A'Begging, Les Fâcheux (new production)

1929   Paris, Berlin, Cologne, London

The Prodigal Son, Le Bal, Le Renard (new production)

Diaghilev dies in Venice

BIBLIOGRAPHY

Alexandre, Arsene — **The Decorative Art of Leon Bakst**
Notes on the Ballets by Jean Cocteau. The Fine Art Society, London 1913. (Original French edition, Brunoff 1913)

Amberg, George — **Art in Modern Ballet**
Pantheon, New York 1946

Astruc, Gabriel — **Le Pavillon de Fantomes**
Grasset, Paris 1929

Barker, Felix — **The House That Stoll Built: The Story of the Coliseum Theatre**
Muller, London 1957

Battersby, Martin — **The Decorative Twenties**
Studio Vista, London 1969

Beaumont, Cyril — **The Diaghilev Ballet in London**
Putnam, London 1946

Benois, Alexandre — **Reminiscences of the Russian Ballet**
Putnam, London 1941
Memoirs
Chatto and Windus, London 1964

Brinson, Peter and Clement Crisp — **Ballet for All**
Pan Books, London 1970

Buckle, Richard — Catalogue for **The Diaghilev Exhibition** 1954/5
In Search of Diaghilev
Sidgwick and Jackson, London 1955
Nijinsky
Weidenfeld and Nicolson, London 1971

Carter, Huntly — **The New Spirit in Drama and Art**
Frank Palmer, London 1912

Cocteau, Jean — **The Journals of Jean Cocteau**
edited by Wallace Fowlie, Museum Press, London 1956

Comœdia Illustré — **Collection des Plus Beaux Numéros des Programmes Consacrés au Ballets et Galas Russes 1909–1921**
Brunoff, Paris 1922

Cooper, Douglas — **Picasso: Theatre**
Weidenfeld and Nicolson, London 1968

Council of Europe — Catalogue for **Les Ballets Russes de Serge de Diaghilev 1909–1929**
Strasbourg 1969

Dolin, Anton — **Autobiography**
Oldbourne, London 1960

Fokine, Michel — **Memoirs of a Ballet Master**
Constable, London 1961

Gray, Camilla — **The Great Experiment: Russian Art 1863–1922**
Thames and Hudson, London 1962

Grigoriev, S. L. — **The Diaghilev Ballet 1909–1929**
Constable, London 1954, Penguin Books 1960

Haskell, Arnold L. — **Balletomania**
Gollancz, London 1934
Diaghileff, His Artistic and Private Life
in collaboration with Walter Nouvel, Gollancz, London 1935

Johnson A. E. — **The Russian Ballet**
Constable, London 1913

Karsavina, Tamara — **Theatre Street**
Heinemann, London 1930

Kerensky, Oleg — **Anna Pavlova**
Hamish Hamilton, London 1973

Kochno, Boris

Le Ballet
Hachette, Paris 1954
Diaghilev and the Ballets Russes
Allen Lane the Penguin Press, London 1971

Levinson, André

Bakst, the Story of the Artist's Life
The Bayard Press, London 1923
The Designs of Léon Bakst for 'The Sleeping Beauty'
Benn Brothers, London 1923

Lieven, Prince

The Birth of the Russian Ballet
Allen and Unwin, London 1936

Lifar, Serge

Diaghilev his Life, his Work and his Legend
Putnam, London 1940
A History of the Russian Ballet
Hutchinson, London 1954

Massine, Léonide

My Life in Ballet
Macmillan, London 1968

Nijinsky, Romola

Nijinsky
Gollancz, London 1933, Penguin Books 1960, Sphere Books 1970

Percival, John

The World of Diaghilev
Studio Vista, London 1971

Propert, W. A.

The Russian Ballet in Western Europe 1909–1920
John Lane The Bodley Head, London 1921
The Russian Ballet 1921–1929
John Lane The Bodley Head, London 1931

Rambert, Marie

Quicksilver
Macmillan, London 1971

Sert, Misia

Two or Three Muses
Museum Press, London 1953

Sitwell, Osbert

The Scarlet Tree
Macmillan, London 1946
Great Morning
Macmillan, London 1948
Laughter in the Next Room
Macmillan, London 1949

Sokolova, Lydia

Dancing for Diaghilev
Murray, London 1960

Spencer, Charles

Erté
Studio Vista, London 1970
Léon Bakst
Academy Editions, London 1973
Catalogue for **The Bakst Exhibition** 1973/4
The Fine Art Society, London

Stravinsky, Igor

Chronicles of My Life
Gollancz, London 1936
Memories and Commentaries with Robert Craft
Faber and Faber, London 1960

Svietlov, Valerien

Le Ballet Contemporain
Brunoff, Paris 1922

Valois, Ninette de

Invitation to the Ballet
John Lane The Bodley Head, London 1937

Wolkonsky, Prince Sergei

My Reminiscences
Hutchinson, London 1925

INDEX

italics refer to illustrations